Conscious Coaching

Conscious Coaching

The Soccer Mom's Bible

Kathleen E. Donovan, MSW

Written in Stone

Orangeburg, South Carolina

First Edition

Published by Written in Stone
            Orangeburg, South Carolina

Manufactured in the United States of America

ISBN 0-9669707-0-5

Library of Congress Catalog Card Number: 99-70858

FOREWORD

I first met Kathy Donovan when she took on the role of coach for my fourth-grade daughter's soccer team, as an unpaid volunteer. Kathy impressed me immediately as an energetic and well-organized coach, with clear standards of performance for herself. She had definite objectives regarding the material she wanted to cover with the girls, and she had a positive image of what it meant to play "as a team." She clearly loved their scrimmages, in which she often participated as enthusiastically as the kids. I had no idea at that time how privileged my daughter's team was to have her as their coach and mentor.

Toward the end of Kathy's first year with our team I suggested to her that she write a book on coaching youth soccer. I felt that my daughter had gained so much maturity, self-discipline, and confidence from her soccer experience that this coach's perspective was worth sharing. I believed, in fact, it had to be shared. Writing a book would be easy, I assured her. Two weeks later, she was fifty pages into the project and I was thoroughly engrossed.

The primary focus of *Conscious Coaching* is the teamwork dynamic. The balance between individual and group concerns, the respect and appreciation of team members for one another, the meaningful responsibilities assigned to players—these are all key elements of Kathy Donovan's self-aware approach to coaching young people. As an anthropologist, I was particularly impressed by the simple communication techniques she used with the team.

Every coach who works with children has a special responsibility. The sport is part of the child's educational experience, in the broadest sense of the word. It is therefore completely inappropriate to introduce into this educational context—as many coaches do—goals and methods that are appropriate in high school and college sports. The central concern always has to be, "What are the kids learning?"— not just about the sport, but about success and failure, about teamwork and individual effort, about their own capabilities in handling stressful situations. As Kathy puts it, "Who are they becoming in the process of playing their sport?"

For this coach, the team doesn't come first. The children do.

—*Clare Wolfowitz, Ph.D.*

PREFACE

At the start of my second season coaching a recreational soccer team, one of my soccer moms, impressed by some of my team management techniques, suggested I write a book on the subject. When I laughed at the thought, she insisted, "I'm serious! This is great material! You write the book and I'll edit it." "God, Clare," I protested. "I'm on a wing and a prayer here. I'm just trying to get through each day."

I had come to coaching from a unique background. Coaching a recreational soccer team was an important step in the process of my recovery from Post-Traumatic Stress Disorder. Three years earlier I had suffered a life-threatening physical assault, which put a violent end to my life as an amateur athlete, a business manager, and a social worker. In addition to chronic musculoskeletal pain and abdominal injuries, the assault left me cognitively disabled, with profound difficulty in concentrating and processing information.

Since all of my symptoms were exacerbated by ordinary social interaction, I made a conscious decision to turn my focus inward. I had lost my health, my intellectual capacity, and my livelihood, but none of these losses equalled forgoing the companionship of my family and friends. It occurred to me one day, as I mourned this conscious separation, that solitude was not a problem but an answer. I would have to trust God's will and allow myself the space and time necessary to heal.

After two years of almost complete social isolation, although I was still fighting to regain my emotional and physical strength, I finally felt able to become more involved with the community. Drawing on my love for children and sports, I accepted the challenge of coaching a girls' soccer team—a challenge that proved to be an exceptional healing experience for me.

In retrospect, I don't know who learned more, the girls or I. The assault and the recovery process had certainly made me a much more conscious coach. Although the team management techniques described in this book were designed specifically to help me manage my symptoms while coaching, it soon became clear that the same techniques also supported the players and helped them focus. In working to bring out the strength in this wonderful group of kids, I recovered my own strength.

—*Kathy Donovan*

DEDICATION

For my Father
who taught me the art of developing consciousness,
the value of recognizing my errors,
and the healing power of forgiveness.
God love you!

ACKNOWLEDGEMENTS

I would like to thank Clare Wolfowitz without whom this book would never have been published. I will be forever grateful to her for inspiring me to write and for investing hour upon hour of her time and creative energy editing, organizing, and restructuring the manuscript. I am most grateful for the friendship we were able to cultivate while working together.

Great appreciation to the players and their parents, managers Lynna Barnes and Betsy King, and three phenomenal coaches: Myron Furbay, Raymond Locke, and Jeff Waldo. I am especially grateful to my niece, Christina, God love her, whose honest feedback and perfect forgiveness have made it a joy to coach her on and off the field. A special thanks to Rachel Abzug who guided me to make a critical decision that allowed our team to close on a very positive note.

Thanks to "Dr. Empathy" (Laurel Northup, MD) for her unwavering support, confidence, and encouragement—for helping me to appreciate that courage is not the absence of fear but rather the commitment to Truth despite great fear, and for encouraging me to always trust my intuition. Thanks also to Diane Heim, Karan Kverno, and Cindy Pearlman. A special thanks to Jim Gorney for providing the avenue through which my treatment team would coach me to a full recovery.

A depth of gratitude to my family for their love and support throughout my life, their great senses of humor, and the very valuable contributions they made to this manuscript.

Great appreciation also to Paul, Sarah, David, and Rachel Wolfowitz for being so patient and generous with me throughout the project.

The contributions, prayers, and healing energy of Mark Diley, Tanya Dunne, Holly Hobough, Deborah Rountree, Shelby Ruddy, Caitlin Parsons, Laurie Gross, James Winbush, Sister Kathleen-Marie Carroll, and Doug Parsons are greatly appreciated.

CONTENTS

Conscious Coaching

The Soccer Mom's Bible

INTRODUCTION
The Conscious Coach

The game is for the kids

I attended a fifth-grade girls' basketball game at which the referee provided an important piece of wisdom.

The parents of one team were, shall I say, *over-involved* in the game. They were constantly yelling at the ref for missing this or that violation. After about ten minutes, while the teams were organizing for a foul shot, the referee took the opportunity to leave the court and address the spectators. "I don't call every violation," he told the parents. "These kids are still learning."

The badgering continued, however. Finally, the ref stopped the game and slowly approached the bleachers. Addressing the coaches and parents of both teams, he said, "Folks, I *know* the game. You don't need to tell me the rules of the game. I don't call every violation because, if I did, I'd be stopping the game every minute and a half. This game is for the kids! They're ten years old! This is not the NBA. They're going to make mistakes. Some I call, some I don't." The ref then walked over to the parent who had been shouting the loudest, and said, "I don't want to hear any more of it. **This is for the kids.**"

Many of the assumptions and attitudes we encounter in youth sports, even in the younger grades, would be more appropriate in the world of competitive athletics. Parents and coaches who look for every competitive advantage, who treat every loss (or tie) as a catastrophe, who feel personally cheated by an unfavorable call—these are people who have forgotten that THE GAME IS FOR THE KIDS. These people would be astonished to realize that, in their passionate involvement in their children's athletics, they are playing a game of their own.

I remember one soccer game when we were trailing the whole time by one point—the score was 1-0. Then, with only two or three minutes remaining, we scored and tied. The girls of the other team were upset and crying when they came over to do the "good game" routine, while our players were almost skipping down the line, they were so pleased.

Then I saw one of the girls of the other team walk up to their coach and say, "Well, we tied!" The coach turned and said to this ten-year old, "Yeah. Tying's a bit like kissing your sister." What a slap in the face for that child! The girl walked away, obviously hurt. She was looking for some support or encouragement, and it wasn't there. These kids know what they have to do, because when they don't do it, they risk getting this kind of treatment from their coach.

In coaching youth teams, the most important question to keep in mind is: *who do the kids become in the process of playing?* Forget what the scoreboard says. Forget about the team ranking. Do our kids become better people by playing their sport? Do they learn to appreciate their teammates, regardless of skill level? Can they support one another? Can they forgive mistakes? Can they set healthy goals for themselves and persevere to achieve them?

This book is the product of an "observation plus trial-and-error" approach to coaching fourth- and fifth-grade kids. It is intended to help parents as they confront some of the problems and decisions that go along with children's sports. Above all, it was written as a way of sharing my own experiences with other coaches, to help fill a need for mutual support and pooled information.

Most of the material in this book comes from my personal journal—problems, successes, and frustrations I experienced coaching a recreational soccer team. All names have been changed to protect individuals' privacy, and the players, parents, and other coaches described are, in most cases, composites of more than one person. Every incident, however, is described as closely as possible to the way things actually transpired.

With few exceptions, I have used the term "girls" (as well as feminine pronouns) when referring to the players—simply because my team was made up of girls—but the information applies to coaching boys too.

Obviously, there can be no single manual we all follow in coaching a group of young people—and if there were, none of us would follow it faithfully. Many times, I confess, I have not been able to follow my own best advice. Every individual coach and player, and every team situation, will be unique. I hope that coaches, parents, and players who read this book will come away with a willingness to try new approaches, develop new techniques of their own, and, above all, observe and learn from the inevitable mistakes we all make in this exciting and rewarding enterprise.

The importance of making mistakes

One of my most interesting experiences as a coach came as a result of one basketball game in which every girl on the team panicked when she got the ball and threw it *to an opponent*. To watch this over and over for an hour was extremely discouraging. After weeks of practicing how to pass, we were still playing hot potato with the ball!

At the practice following this fateful game, we began as always with a team meeting, gathered in a semi-circle to discuss our performance. I asked the team, "How many of us passed to an opponent during the game?" A few of the girls grinned, shrugged their shoulders, giggled a little, and raised their hands. I asked the question again, "Come on, how many of us passed to the other team?" A few more girls scanned their teammates and, with a little more embarrassment now, raised their hands. "O.K. Keep your hands up everyone. How many of the rest of you panicked and passed the ball to the other team? Be really honest with yourselves and your team." With almost painful reluctance, a few more girls raised their hands. This left only two out of the eleven-member team.

Looking straight at these last two, who were sitting side by side, I tried again. "Who else passed the ball to the other team? Come on now, it looks like the whole team did it." One of the two holdouts crossed her arms in front of her and gave a very emphatic shake of her head, "Not me." In fact, these last two were by far the worst offenders!

This presented me with an opportunity to use the team experience as a metaphor for life. I raised the question, "What happens if we deny the mistakes we make?" Ten-year-old girls love to talk about what they're thinking, and hands went up everywhere to offer several important ideas. The conclusion was obvious to all of us: by refusing to admit a mistake, players would continue to make that same mistake.

"So then," I continued, "what's the difference between a mistake and a behavior?" Their eagerness to respond surprised me. They could hardly stay seated, each one begging to be heard. "A behavior is something you do all the time, and a mistake is something you only do once or twice," one girl offered. "If we deny that we've made a mistake, won't it become our behavior?" I asked the group.

I looked around at their perplexed faces and moved ahead. "This is not just about basketball passes, this is about life. Every day, people point out errors to us, at school, church, home, and on a team. These situations are actually opportunities," I told them, "to grow and change and become better people. Imagine if something you did or said really hurt a friend, and she told you about it and you denied it. You just couldn't accept that you had done something harmful. You'll probably do it again and again, until it becomes your way, your behavior. What would happen then?" "You'll lose your friends," someone said. "It's not easy," I summed up, "to have people point out our errors, or to be able to accept them, but it's a whole lot harder to go through life turning our mistakes into behaviors."

My first (and best) coach was my dad. Many times, when I was down a couple of games in tennis and beginning to lose interest and give up, I would hear my dad say from across the net, "The battle's never over till the last shot is fired." Sometimes I wanted to scream when he said that, but more often those words encouraged me to forget the last few blunders and just play the next point. I can still remember the first few times I made great shots and scored after hearing those words. "God, he's right," I thought. "It really works if I just think about one point at a time."

His cajoling me to stay in the present moment was helping me do my best with each point. He was also interrupting the destructive habit of giving in to discouragement. It's very easy to let our mistakes lead us into sabotaging ourselves. I can remember hitting a ball into the net and getting so angry with myself I deliberately hit it into the net again! This was my confirmation that I was just a lousy tennis player, that it wasn't a good day for me, I couldn't do anything right, and I'm a lousy person. This is where self-deprecation inevitably ends up: "I'm a lousy person."

I was fortunate to have the same wonderful coach for fifteen years. I began playing tennis at the age of five or six, and I played regularly through college. My dad's consistent guidance carried over into my everyday life as well. "Just stay in the present moment and take each point as it comes," he'd say. Like everyone else, I can get really down on myself after a few bad experiences, but I can also very quickly focus on the next point and allow myself to appreciate my successes.

Most importantly, my dad never "beat up on me" over my mistakes. He never stood on the other side of the net and asked, "Why did you do that?" He never yelled at me to do better or to do something differently. Instead, he took every opportunity to instruct, to point out my mistakes, and to make me aware of what I needed to change in order to improve. He was always respectful and calm in his approach. I was fortunate to have a coach whose corrections were never more humiliating than the mistake. He could tell me what I did wrong, demonstrate the correct way, have me repeat what he had shown me, and go right back to playing.

⊛   My dad didn't have to resort to badgering or verbal abuse because *I was not an extension of his ego.* He recognized that I was a completely separate person, whose mistakes in no way reflected on him.

The most important lesson I learned from my dad was to forgive myself and move on. I decided if my coach could excuse my faults, surely others could too. I never had to feel guilty for disappointing my coach, nor did he diminish my accomplishments by taking credit for my skill.

The coach's role
• *The coach as critic*
    The way a coach calls attention to mistakes is a major factor in the team's development. It's easy to tell if your way of dealing with mistakes is facilitating the team's growth or destructive to it. Do the players feel free to ask for individual help or clarification on specific drills? Often, I see kids trying to point out to their teammates the correct way to do something, or one player will ask another for help. It's a good sign when they approach the coach directly, or respond to a correction with "Wait. Can you stay and watch me to see if I do it right?" That's when you know they're not afraid of making a mistake—they understand that learning is a cooperative process.

I have made the mistake of getting so focused on having everyone on the team master a particular skill I'm unable to accept the fact that some of the kids just aren't going to get it that day. That's when I can become impatient and condescending, perhaps even humiliating. "This skill is on the agenda for today," I tell myself, "and by God they're all going to learn it if it kills me." And, every time, this attitude does in fact "kill me," and the team's spirit, for an entire practice.

I was extremely frustrated one day, trying to teach the team how to step on the soccer ball, then reverse direction and take the ball away with the opposite foot. It is a difficult skill to teach and a real challenge to master, as it involves reversing directions with a change of feet. About half of the girls got it and were practicing on their own, while the other half was still confused.

Instead of recognizing this was one of those drills that some would get the first time and others would not, I decided they would *all* master it, even if it took the entire practice time to do it. I singled out the ones who were still confused, the anger rising in my voice, "You step on the ball with the right foot, hop over, turn to the left, and take away with the left foot!"

Pretty soon, I saw shoulders drawing in and up, jaws clenching—and then total shutdown. The kids became unwilling to try anything for fear of being further embarrassed. The most painful part of this experience was knowing the girls weren't shutting down to annoy me—they just couldn't get it. Shutting down was the only way to get the message across to me.

I left practice that day completely exasperated, but I had to ask myself, "Why couldn't I just let it go? Why did I have to keep drilling this, to the point where they couldn't take in any more information?" I needed to look carefully at the mistakes I was making as a coach.

After much thought, I realized that I too have considerable difficulty with these types of tasks: distinguishing right from left, reversing directions, and storing sequential information long enough to mimic an observed action. Things that were once extremely easy for me, such as observing a skill and performing it almost immediately, became nearly impossible for me in the aftermath of the assault. These girls had been mirroring my own inadequacies. How dare they show me so clearly my own terrible handicap!

That day at soccer practice I was forced to take a look at myself—one-half of the team representing the Kathy that once was, and the other half the Kathy I am today. My frustration resulted not from the girls' inability to grasp the skill but from the feelings triggered inside me.

At the following practice I did the same drill again using a less demanding approach and received positive results. This time I just said, "Do your best and eventually you'll get it." It took several weeks, but almost all of them mastered it. I was as proud of their success as they were.

• *The coach as teacher: "Let's stand corrected."*

An underlying conflict of philosophy with Dave, my co-coach, presented itself when I took on the problem of Sylvia's recurrent babyish behavior at practices. In spite of her clear athletic ability, Sylvia tended to giggle and fool around constantly during drills. She paid no attention to our explanations and reacted to criticism by retreating into herself.

Every time Dave or I tried to correct her, Sylvia would giggle, draw in her shoulders, drop her torso and face, and curl her arms in as if protecting herself. She appeared to shrink almost a foot, curled up as if in a standing fetal position. She would regress right before our eyes with every correction we made. To a simple correction like "Let's try to use the instep and not the toe to kick the ball," her response would be "I know, but . . ." There was always some kind of excuse. As long as she remained defensive, Sylvia could not hear our corrections, and she'd continue to make the same mistakes.

Other girls on the team occasionally responded in the same defensive way, laughing anxiously when given a correction and coming up with reasons for not doing what they were supposed to do ("I didn't see Katie so I *couldn't* pass to her"). At ten, they're going through physical changes, and there are much greater demands on them in school, and in some cases at home, and some of them aren't ready for it all. When the stress is too great they sometimes lapse into "baby talk."

Though Sylvia wasn't the only one with this defensive reaction, she especially was debilitated by it. I had tried all sorts of approaches, such as introducing the instruction each time with, "This is just a correction." At several practices I had taken Sylvia aside to talk with her, to tell her how much she's capable of and what I needed her to do to cooperate— in other words, to pump her up a bit. Nothing worked.

At about that time in my own game of soccer I happened to experience the same problem, but from a different perspective. I was playing with a new forward who was not as fast as my usual partner (someone I could count on every time to get a leading pass). As midfielder, I would make passes but Beth, the new forward, couldn't get to them in time. I began holding on to the ball longer—which is a problem I have anyway. At halftime, Beth came up to me, clearly upset, and said, "Hey, Kathy. Get rid of the ball one dribble sooner." She was evidently containing her frustration, and I just said, "Okay."

All sorts of reasons relating to what was happening on the field went through my mind at that moment, but why stop to explain myself, I wondered, and give Beth the impression that I'm not hearing what she said? She went on to say, "It looks as if you're going to be able to get around them, but you can't, and they're stealing the ball from you, so get rid of the ball one dribble sooner." I said, "Okay, no problem. I'll try to change that." And that's what I decided to focus on for the rest of the game.

I realized then it had taken me about thirty-six years to get to the point that I could "stand corrected," without the ifs, ands, or buts. In fact, I encounter adults every day who have not yet arrived at that point—who have not learned how powerful it can be to hear a correction, acknowledge it, and work on making use of it. The typical response for most of us, whether we're on a soccer field, in a classroom, or in an office, is to start defending ourselves, to try to explain why we did the things we did.

The fact is, throughout our lives there will be times when other people point out our mistakes—or show us ways to improve and grow. This kind of coaching can be a great help if we learn to appreciate it and make use of it—rather than hear it as criticism and reject it.

Coming home from that game I kept thinking, When I'm being corrected out on the field, I can respond, "Okay, gotcha." Why can't I get the kids to do that? Isn't it part of the coach's job to help the kids hear the corrections?

At the next practice I said to the whole team, "I get very, very frustrated when I attempt to correct you, because some of you cannot hear the correction. You're busy defending yourselves as soon as I start to correct you, even before I've said what I want to say. You offer an explanation before you've even heard what the problem is! If you can't hear the correction, you'll never make the change. Some of you are doing this." I drew my shoulders in, crossed my arms in front of me, and dropped my head forward (giving my impression of Sylvia's "fetal position"). "Am I getting smaller or bigger?" I asked. They all laughed and said, "Smaller, much smaller!" I looked at them and said, "This is you when we correct you. You're telling us that the correction is too much for you—but it's really not.

"How about now?" I asked, straightening my body and looking directly ahead. "Bigger!" they yelled. "It takes a big person to take criticism," I told them, "to really make use of criticism to improve and grow. I want you to remember that the next time Dave or I correct you. Have any of you heard the expression 'I stand corrected?'" One girl raised her hand. "*This* is standing corrected," I said as I planted my feet on the ground. "My feet are firmly planted, my legs are straight, my chin is up." I stood erect and looked at each girl in turn. "You stand tall with your spine straight, you look the person in the eye as they're telling you what they want and what they think you need to change. Then you nod and say, 'Okay, I've got it. Thanks!' That is standing corrected—with no buts, no excuses. And then you make your correction.

"So, from now on, if you start to defend yourself after being corrected, I will just say, 'Can we stand corrected for this one?' or 'Let's stand corrected.' When you hear that, it's your cue to straighten up, look me in the eye, and say, 'Okay, I've got it.' It's your cue to focus on what we're saying to you. We want you to focus on improving—not on the mistake.

"One other thing: I am acutely aware that my tone of voice is often disrespectful, and that my own frustration comes out in a condescending tone that belittles you at times—which may be the reason you are retreating from correction. And if that's the case, what can you say to me?" One girl responded, "We could say 'Excuse me.'" "Okay, then say, 'Excuse me, Kathy, can you say that another way?' or just, 'Kathy, can you say that again?' That will be my cue that I have to change my words or tone of voice to help you make a correction."

After the girls went home that day, I said to Dave, "I've got to find a way to reach her. It's primarily for Sylvia that I'm trying this, but the whole team can benefit from learning how to stand corrected." Dave's response sounded almost angry: "You realize, don't you, that you're trying to change the personality of the kid? We're soccer coaches. We ought to be able to come out here and expect the kids to play soccer. That's all we're here for! We're coaches! We're not here to change their personalities or their behavior."

I was a bit shocked by what felt like an attack. My own instincts told me that, as coaches, we need to work on this issue of *coachability*. The alternative was to drop the less coachable girls from the team. In my view, our primary responsibility is to the kids as people, not as soccer players— and most of them benefit hugely from participating in team sports. I answered, "If it's going to help her play better soccer, then I'm going to do it. I'm willing to try anything to bring out her athletic ability, so she can realize her potential as a person."

"Well, I'm just not sure that's what we're supposed to be doing," Dave responded. "That's a lot more than we should be doing."

After that conversation, I began to question myself severely. Maybe I should be focusing only on their ball skills and where we stand in the league. Maybe I was trying to do too much. Maybe teaching life skills is out of bounds. Maybe coaching should just be teaching the game of soccer and that's it.

This episode of soul searching had a nice, neat ending. At the start of the next practice, I took a moment to review "standing corrected" so the team would know what to expect. Sylvia didn't seem to need the reminder. She came to practice early, dressed in soccer clothes, looking like a real athlete (which I hadn't seen from her before). She immediately got out her gear and started pumping up her ball. Before I knew it, she was pumping up the other players' balls too.

The metaphor was irresistible. I had been trying for

weeks to pump this girl up with pep talks, and now—after that simple talk about standing corrected—she had come to practice pumped up. That day, she participated in every drill without the silliness, showing just how impressive her athletic skills could be. During that practice I must have corrected her a dozen times, and not once did she giggle, laugh, curl her body up, or retreat into baby talk. She would turn, look at me, and say, "Okay." In fact, toward the end of practice, when we were doing throws, she called me off to the side and asked, "Kathy, is this right? Wait, is this one right?" Sylvia was actually asking for guidance in learning a technique!

And she wasn't the only one. Diane was corrected by Dave in the middle of scrimmage (we sometimes stop a play to point out a player's options at a particular moment). She began to reach for an excuse, slouched with her hands together, squirming. I was standing right behind her, watching and I said, "Hey, let's just try to stand corrected for this, okay?" She turned toward me, gave a big smile, stood straight, and said, "Okay. Okay." After that day, Diane looked me right in the face whenever I gave her a correction.

After that practice I asked Dave, "What did you think of Sylvia today?" I wanted to make sure the change I was seeing was actually there. Dave said, "Yeah, she did really well. I've got to hand it to you this time, Kathy. I'm impressed. You had the right approach with Sylvia, and she really appreciates it."

"Stand corrected" is a successful verbal cue, much like those described in chapter two. It gives the player a safe way to hear corrections, to shift her focus away from herself and onto the behavior on which she needs to work. This is a lesson that will benefit the kids in every area of activity in the future—in high school and college, in their jobs, in competitive athletics, in family life, and in the volunteer work they do. It's not really a matter of changing their personalities—

it's just trying to bring out the best in them, helping them let go of behaviors that are not adaptive.

• *Making a difference*

The coaches in my own life—in addition to my father, who was truly extraordinary—have included teachers, employers, and a very special Sister of Mercy, Sr. Kathleen Marie Carroll. These are the people who did not accept some of my behavior and coached me to make changes that would serve me in positive ways. When I was fifteen, I'm sure most teachers would have given up on me and my bad attitude, but my English teacher, Ms. Gross, saw something in me and she worked really hard to help me see the best in myself. I will be forever grateful for that. When I was giving up on myself, that's when she tried the hardest to help me. I shudder to think what path my life might have taken had she not been there for me at fifteen.

With ten-year olds, that kind of support is equally important, and coaches and teachers have a responsibility to work hard to provide it. For me, working with kids who need help in appreciating themselves is a way of giving something back, a way of acknowledging the people who have coached me when I needed it. Failing to try to bring out that potential—to simply accept the child's self-evaluation—is, to me, almost a crime.

CHAPTER ONE
The Team Triangle

There are three components to every youth team: the coach (or coaches), the players, and the players' parents. The dignity of the team rests on a relationship of mutual respect among these three components. This means dealing with decisions and problems as partners, sharing power rather than competing for power, and always keeping in mind the team's primary goal: aiding the development of all team members.

⊛   Coach, players, and parents form what I call "the team triangle."

The balance between the interests of the individual player and those of the team can be a delicate matter. Problems consistently arise in two areas: (1) the player's desire to play a particular position versus the team's most effective use of each player, and (2) a player's schedule conflict versus the team's requirement that players attend practices and games. The solution seems simple and straightforward: playing on the team means a reasonable commitment to attend practices and games (barring the occasional emergency absence) and to accept the coach's decisions. This formula works well *as long as the coach is consistent and fair* in deciding such issues as position and playing time. A coach's unfair decisions can do more damage to the team than any amount of complaining by players.

In certain areas the interests of the player must come first. In any case involving physical injury or psychological damage, the team and the coach need to support the player, rather than the reverse. It is ultimately up to the parents to ensure that their children's physical and psychological well-being is always a primary concern. One important aim of this book is to help parents make this crucial judgment call.

Supporting the coach

A coach working alone has a huge and very exhausting job. However experienced and effective the coach may be, a team of twelve or more kids is too large to allow individual attention to all players unless there is an assistant. If team members are under the age of twelve, the group is probably too unruly to work with unless you can divide them up into drill teams—which, again, requires some assistance.

The assistant coach may be a mature high school student or an actively participating parent. If necessary, parents can assist at practices on a rotating basis, though a single assistant coach is preferable for the sake of consistency. The assistant coach—whether a parent or a high school student—must be committed to the activity and follow the same guidelines for attendance set for the players. There may be times, of course, that it's advantageous to the team to bring in an outsider as a guest assistant or trainer.

⚽ To prevent confusion the coach must communicate ahead of time exactly what is expected of the assistant coach, guest assistant, or trainer.

In addition to an assistant coach, it's essential to have a parent serve as team manager, to handle administrative matters such as practice fields, telephone calls, registration, and snack assignments. This job too can be shared with an assistant manager.

A co-coach arrangement can work beautifully, with two people sharing charge of the team. This arrangement requires especially good communication skills, so that both coaches understand the division of responsibility. I have had the privilege of working with three very different and talented people, as co-coach, head coach, and assistant coach. I have learned a great deal from them, as I hope I have made clear in every chapter of this book. I know I could not have managed even a week of practices without their support.

Parents

The parents' role is the least defined of the three elements of the team triangle. Parents tend not to see themselves as part of the team organization, and there is generally little opportunity for them to participate as a group with coherent interests. Perhaps that is why parents often seem so passive in dealing with team issues.

Parents need to take an active role on the team. They need to recognize that the coach does not know everything. It's fine to serve as coach's assistant—lending a hand in managing, skill development, etc.—but in basic questions of conduct, parents have to keep coaches in check, just as coaches need to keep parents in check.

⚽   The kids can help keep us all in check, but only if we listen to them, and if we provide a safe avenue for them to provide constructive criticism.

Parent problems
• *Parents vs. parents*

When parents are able to cheer for other players on the team as well as for their own kids, it's terrific. It sometimes has more meaning for a child when another parent is cheering for her. It's equally powerful—in a negative way—when players are reprimanded by parents other than their own.

My brother told me about watching a game in which his son Dan was playing, when a teammate's father reprimanded Dan. "He just said, 'Stay with the ball,'" my brother recalled, "but it sounded to me like criticism. There was kind of an angry tone. I wasn't sure about it, so I didn't say anything. Soon after that he did say, 'Way to go, Dan.' But I'm still not sure about that initial comment."

A parent on my team confessed to me one day that she was pretty upset with another parent who was correcting her daughter. She said, "If I want to correct my daughter, I'll correct my daughter; and if the coach wants to correct my daughter, then the coach will correct my daughter. But I won't have another parent correcting her." It's often offensive to parents when their child's mistakes or inadequacies are pointed out by another parent.

⚽   A clear communication from the coach may be needed to solve the problem of parents correcting children other than their own.

The conversation with my brother happened to take place just before our own team meeting when we discussed the general problem of coaching—by both parents and coaches—from the sidelines (see chapter two). This was a problem identified by the players, who found it distracting, and sometimes confusing, to hear instructions yelled from the sidelines.

The fact is, most parents don't know the game well enough to offer useful criticism or corrections to their own children, let alone to other kids on the team. Nevertheless, the role of expert authority seems to carry over from years of serving as the child's primary life coach. The parents are so used to having the answers, they find it difficult to adjust to a situation in which they lack the necessary expertise to give instruction to their children.

⚽   Before the next game, I made a point of telling the parents that their kids need no correcting or reprimanding from them during the game, and that their doing so was usually detrimental. I said, "We need you at our games, and we need you to cheer for us. We're all in this together, so it's important that we don't tear each other down."

• *Parents and coaches*

We played against one team whose coach was screaming at his players—as, unfortunately, we all do sometimes—to get into this or that position, move forward, or move back. At one point he was trying to get his defense to move forward: "Come up, come up! Move up, move up!" Finally his anger erupted. "Move up, Laurie! Goddamit, I said move up!" One of my mothers came over to me and said, "I can't believe the way he's talking to those kids!"

I try to avoid saying things about other coaches to the parents, because I would sure hate it if somebody videotaped me! But when the mother repeated to me what the coach said, I was shocked. I would be curious to know whether the parents of his players customarily let him get away with using that kind of language to their fourth graders.

The dynamic between parents and coach is frequently a problem. Either the parents are trying to direct the coach, or the coach is behaving questionably and not being called on it. Coaches are bullied by parents and parents are bullied by coaches.

Ideally, the relationship should be cooperative. The coach has committed a sizable chunk of time to the team and should have final say about practice times, positions, and rules for practices. However, parents can be very helpful in bringing things to the coach's attention. In the situation with Laurie, for example, her mother might have said to the coach, "You really shook up the kids" or "I wonder how Laurie felt when you said that to her." Make the coach more aware of his actions. The coach has a responsibility to handle the job fairly and without causing damage to the children. The parents have the responsibility to see that the coach behaves appropriately.

As members of the team, the parents are being coached by the coaches and by their children. In turn, the coach needs to be *coached* by the parents. Putting all the power in the hands of one person creates an impossible situation. We're all going to make mistakes, sometimes huge ones, but if they are pointed out to us, we can change the action before a pattern of behavior is formed. If a coach is behaving in a questionable manner and the parents don't point it out, the misstep will surely lead to a pattern of behavior—and it will eventually become the dynamic between the coach and the players. Remember, it's easier to bring about a change if the parents speak up early on, when their concerns first arise, rather than later when the problem has reached crisis proportion.

My major complaint about parents is not that they are too critical of the coach—though it may feel that way sometimes—but that they are not critical enough. I know how I feel about my niece, and if she were being mistreated by an abusive coach for whatever reason, I would certainly say something: "Did you hear what you just said to my niece?" or "I noticed you used these words when you spoke to Caitlin. Isn't there a better way of talking to her?" or "It seems as if you don't like my niece." And if I saw consistent favoritism toward her, I would feel compelled to say something about that too.

⚽   The most constructive approach is for parents to point out problems at each step along the way: "I wonder if you've thought about . . ." This is a matter of communication—how to bring up unpleasant business in a respectful way. A really serious situation, of course, may need to be brought up more sternly.

There also seems to be something about sports that compels some parents to drop the self-control they normally exercise in front of their children, or in a professional setting, and indulge a kind of belligerent rage in interacting with the coach. What kind of example are they setting for their children? Why do they feel it is more acceptable to scream at their child's coach than at her doctor or her teacher?

At one memorable game, our team had a penalty kick, right in front of the goalie box. I was at the fifty-yard mark getting my substitutes organized to go in, and I didn't see what was happening on the field. An irate parent yelled, "Coach! Coach! You've got a kick! Who do you want to take the kick?" The anger in his voice caused me to freeze. It took me a few seconds to realize what was going on. Our team had a nice, fat penalty kick and he felt his daughter, a powerful kicker, ought to be taking it. By the time I yelled out to the girls, "Shari takes the kick," Ellen, my weak kicker, was giving it her best shot. (This was the incident that taught me to specify ahead of time how penalty kicks would be handled.)

Needless to say, we didn't score, though Ellen obviously tried her best. "O.K., Ellen, good try!" I called out to her as I began to walk down the sidelines. Shari's dad, however, was too angry to let it go, and he followed me, yelling, "You're the coach! You have to pay attention to the game! You can't be talking to people on the sidelines!" This harangue rattled me, much the way a player might be rattled by being berated by a coach or parent. It's best for parents to refrain from coaching the coach during games—but when they feel it's necessary, they too need to observe the basic rules of respectful coaching.

⊛   This incident prompted me to reiterate clearly, to all the parents, my original policy statement: there could be no yelling—*ever*—either at coaches or referees, if I was to remain the team's coach.

• *Disciplining the coach*

The extreme scenario of parent–coach problems was reported by a parent with a traveling team of ten-year olds. "You're not going to believe what happened at the tournament," Dolores said.

Delores had not been present, but had been told that one of the fathers got into a screaming match with the coach. "The coach ended up slapping the father," she continued, "and then head-butted him!"

I said, "Why didn't someone call the police and have the coach arrested for assault?!" Dolores agreed that would have been appropriate, but she guessed the men wouldn't take that approach for fear of appearing weak. "At the very least," I said, "the coach should be banned from coaching! No one should tolerate this."

That particular soccer club has an executive board consisting of four fathers and one mother. The board members discussed the issue and decided the coach would not be allowed to coach the last game—but he could coach the game the following week. "Why was that the decision?" I asked. "Well," Dolores explained, "this next game is a really important one, against a tough team." "So," I offered, "we're still giving the message to the kids that the scoreboard is more important than what they're learning." "Yes," Dolores agreed.

"I feel this is a moral dilemma," she went on, "and the kids shouldn't play. But the other parents say that if we stop the kids from playing, it's punishing them and not the coach." "Indeed it is," I responded. "That's why the coach should be punished. The coach should be held responsible for his behavior. The kids didn't commit that assault." Delores said she could understand someone getting angry or losing control. She could even forgive the slap itself—although it is, of course, unacceptable. What she couldn't tolerate, she said, is that the coach never apologized to the parent he struck, and never held a parent meeting to say, "I'm sorry for what I did and I'll never do it again."

It seems clear that both the screaming parent and the violent coach were out of control and out of line. Parents need to take the initiative. As a group, they need to say to the coach and to the offending parent, "This is not acceptable behavior. We will not have you setting this kind of example for our children. We will not have our children learning that this unsportsmanlike conduct is tolerated."

There is strength in numbers. After all, there's one coach and there are twenty to thirty parents. Surely, twenty parents can form a group and get the message across. In this case, however, the decision by the board was a *show* of discipline. Obviously, the team's record mattered more to those parents than what they were teaching their children.

A big part of a parent's job is teaching his or her kids to control their behavior within acceptable bounds. It's important that the people teaching our children, including athletic coaches, are able to control their *own* destructive impulses.

⊛ Imagine seeing a coach strike a parent, and then allowing that coach to teach your child! Parents routinely put up with derogatory, abusive, damaging conduct on the part of coaches that they would never tolerate in the schools.

How did parents become so spineless in the area of sports education? If a teacher struck a parent, he'd be out of a job. Parents would rally together if such a teacher were not severely disciplined, and the matter would be made public. But in team sports, the chance of winning a trophy short-circuits the disciplinary process—*we've got to have that trophy!*

• *Parents and players: joining a team*

I feel that all parents should encourage children to participate in something—*anything*—athletic, from the time they're young—if only for the sake of a team experience they won't get anywhere else. Richard Barnes, co-author of *The Soccer Mom's Handbook*, points out that soccer is an ideal beginner's sport because the basic skills are not difficult, it's highly aerobic, and all positions are more or less equal in importance.

On the first day of my first coaching job, one of the girls showed up late and didn't seem to know anyone. She did not want to participate in any of the drills, and when it came time to scrimmage, she didn't want to be on either team.

Finally, Emily agreed to play defense on my side. She stood off by herself, hands jammed in her pockets, completely rigid, with a look on her face that could kill. She was obviously angry. I walked over to her and said, "You don't really want to be here, do you?" She shook her head, and I said, "You're kind of being forced to be here, right?" She said, "Yes," and I asked, "If you could have your choice of where you would be right now, where would it be?" "I wanted to play baseball!" she said, and she started to cry. The ball came toward her and she kicked it away, still crying. When she had quieted just a little, I asked, "So baseball is what you like?" "Yes!" "Well, how come you're not playing baseball?" "Because my Mom won't let me!" she said, as she started to cry again.

By late in the season, Emily was a different kid—standing on the sidelines with her teammates, begging, "Can I go in now?" The changes in her were obvious, on the field and off. She bonded with the others, made friends, and ended up loving the game.

Similarly, my sister forced my niece, Caitlin, to join a soccer team when she was just starting fourth grade. Caitlin felt very out of place. All the kids on the team knew one another and she didn't know anyone. She had never played soccer and had none of the skills. You could see that she was uncomfortable and didn't know what to do. In fact, none of the girls did, but Caitlin naturally assumed that everybody else knew what to do because they had played before. Watching the games, her parents would see her standing back and they would call to her, "Move, Caitlin! Go! Go!" She clearly didn't like it.

After the second game, my sister was upset to the point of tears about the situation. She didn't know whether she was doing the right thing, forcing her daughter to play soccer. I didn't know if she was doing the right thing either. My honest feeling was, "Why force a kid into this?" But watching Caitlin through the season, I began to see that it had been a wise decision.

Caitlin would never have discovered soccer on her own and would never have taken the initiative to join a team, yet she is benefiting in a number of ways. She is gaining confidence in herself and her skills. She is able to negotiate with team members. And she now knows she is capable of comprehending what the coach is directing her to do.

I urge parents of children like Caitlin to commit to a few seasons, if possible on the same team with the same coach (provided the coach is working well with the kids). Then they can make a decision, together with the child, about whether to stay with the game. In most cases, the child will want to continue.

The experience turned out to be a very positive one for Caitlin. She told me, "In the beginning, Aunt Kathy, I hated it. I'm just not into sports, it's not me. But I'm lucky, because I happened to like playing soccer." Caitlin will never be a competitive soccer player, but she's going to be able to stay with this for a while and have fun with it.

There are other kids who simply lack ball skills, as well as the interest in developing them. If their parents want them to participate in an athletic activity, there is a wide range of non-ball activities that provide exercise, such as martial arts and dance, which might be more appealing to them.

Parents need to be clear, however, about their motives in pushing a child to play sports. In a family I know, the father is insisting that his daughter go to a higher level team— he's actually forcing her to play soccer. Ginnie not only lacks skill, she has absolutely no interest in playing the sport. Nevertheless, her dad is pushing her into a more competitive level of play. (Most soccer organizations distinguish between two or more levels of play. Competitive teams require try-outs, usually hold longer or more frequent practices than recreational teams, and demand more attention to specific skills.) This father, like many others, appears to be living vicariously through his daughter. Why not recognize that she has gone as far as she wants to in this particular sport, that she's happy with recreational play and with being a pretty good player on her team? Parents sometimes push their kids to a more competitive level because it's something they want, not something the child wants.

Why should playing on a recreational team have a negative connotation? If the child is enjoying the sport at that level, I encourage parents to counsel her to stay with it rather than push for more competitive play. She can enjoy the activity the way most adults enjoy tennis or golf, as a social activity. It may be helpful for parents to get together and share their perspectives on what's best for their children.

⊛   A friend summed it up this way: "If I saw a daughter of mine playing with the soccer ball in the backyard all the time, really showing an interest in the sport, I would get her into soccer camps and other activities to give her the best opportunity to realize her goals. But if she's not showing that kind of interest, she may be better off as a recreational player."

• *Parents and players: excessive pressure*

Pressure is excessive when a particular player feels it is excessive. One of the players on Caitlin's soccer team would become furious every time her parents said anything to her from the sidelines during a game. She might be dribbling down the field and she'd hear her mother or father yell something—even "Go!"—and she would come to a dead stop, put her foot on the ball, turn to her parents and scream, "SHUT UP!" This was her very straightforward way of handling what she felt as excessive pressure. It wasn't long before her parents got the message and stopped saying anything from the sidelines. For the time being, at least, there was no way they could express their support for their daughter except by remaining silent.

A friend of mine told me about her son's soccer team, a fourth-grade boys' recreational team. They lost almost every game. One of the players on the team is a big, tough kid, very aggressive, and a very good player. When he gets hurt on the field, however, he stays down. My friend is sure the boy doesn't want to get up because he is crying. His father is "a tough guy" and does not allow that kind of "weakness" in his son. So when the boy gets hurt, he stays down with his head buried in the field. Then, when he has gained control, he gets up and continues playing.

This boy's father once gave a little speech to my friend, insisting that "It's not important whether they win or lose as long as they're having a good time out here. It's just a game." Later on in the season, however, he announced, "I'm not coming to these games anymore. They never win." And he stopped coming to the games. He decided to look for a "better team" for his son because "I don't want him on this losing team." This father, through his actions, is telling his son he can't enjoy watching him play or take delight in his progress if his team isn't winning its games. He's giving the message that his son has to win in order to be something in his father's eyes.

Parents have to remain sensitive to their kids' needs and desires. Excessive pressure doesn't make them better athletes. It can, however, make them fearful and unhappy.

• *Parents and referees*

I watched a game in which the parents of one team could not accept a referee's call. Their team scored a goal, but when the ref blew the whistle and called, "Offsides," the goal did not count. This sent the parents into an uproar, screaming, "What's the matter, ref?!" Someone in the crowd finally called out, "Offsides."

Nobody seemed to know what offsides was, so I explained the rule to those around me. (This can be a tricky call, but basically an offensive player is offside if she is closer to the opponent's goal when the ball is played to her than the opposing team's last defending player.) "That's a stupid rule!" one mother shouted—and she once again began screaming at the ref! The other parents joined in berating the ref: "That's ridiculous! What kind of a rule is that?!"

There was a sense of contagion about the initial outburst, and before long other spectators on that side of the field—adults—began yelling at the ref, on a call they clearly knew nothing about. Even when they learned there was, in fact, a rule on which he based the call (a rule that has been part of soccer since the beginning of the game!), this did not calm the tide of protest.

⊕   This kind of anger has nothing to do with the game. There's no call, in any game, that justifies the kind of rage I have sometimes witnessed on the sidelines.

When I attended another team's tournament games, I observed that when the coach yelled at the ref, the parents yelled at the ref. The parents never yelled at the ref if the coach didn't yell first. It may be that the parents are trying to show the coach, "We're with you!"

I have been told that there is a division of opinion among parents on this team regarding their coach. The coach's supporters obviously feel the need to support him vocally in his opinions on the ref's calls, much like members of a political party.

Sitting on the sidelines, coaches and parents can't see everything. The refs don't see everything either, but they do the best they can—and it's their job to referee, not ours.

Coach problems

A friend of mine, a former girls' softball coach, asked me, "Do you have any favorites?" I was very surprised by this question, since I had assumed that anyone in authority— coach, teacher, or manager—who had a favorite charge would not be conscious of it. I thought for a moment and said that while I didn't think so, it would be interesting to know how the players on my team felt. I explained that they are all very different, and the challenge is trying to reach each individual. My friend told me about a pitcher on her softball team who was so extraordinary in her pitching skills, considering her young age, that "it was hard not to give her extra attention."

My friend and I were clearly not on the same page with what we understood would be the reason behind having a favorite. I immediately thought about the *individual personalities* that made up our team, while she was looking at *individual athletic skills*.

• Coachability

An important part of coaching is recognizing and working with the individual personalities that make up any team. I have found, through years of management and teaching experience, that there's always a way to reach a child—although it may not be my way. If I can look at the person as a unique individual without comparing her to anyone else (including myself), I can always find a way to help her get beyond the problem we're facing, allowing her to realize her inner strength and express her own soul's glory.

Mark Diley, a PGA golf pro for over twenty years, reports similar experiences. When he first started to teach golf, he told me, he expected everyone to learn the same way he learned. This was not a very productive assumption, and before long he developed a few different approaches to teaching. Now, he says, he has a very different perspective. He sees every new student as "carrying a lock," and his job is to find the right key on his ever-growing ring of keys to "unlock" that student's abilities.

I've faced a number of "locked" students myself. The most challenging was a young Japanese girl I tutored. Tomoko had become increasingly frustrated with the experience of adapting to an American school, and at the time I met her she was dealing with her frustrations by "shutting down." Whenever she encountered a problem, she would refuse to speak, bury her face, and finally burst into tears.

I learned to recognize when she was beginning to shut down, and at the first sign of frustration I would suggest taking a break. We would stop what we were working on, and I would assure her we did not have to keep going. At first, this meant the lesson was over at that point. I had to assure Tomoko's parents that we were on the right course, even though I wasn't certain how it would work out. It seemed essential to me that Tomoko feel she have some sense of control over our session.

After following this course of action a few sessions, she was able to take a break and then ask to continue. Within a few weeks, when Tomoko got frustrated she would simply take a deep breath, brace herself, and move ahead with the lesson. It was wonderful to see this child go from utter despair to taking charge of herself.

All coaches recognize the "coachable" athlete—but how many of *us* are truly coachable in our job as coach? Can we learn from each player a new method of coaching, one that works for that individual? A coachable player is not necessarily one who adapts to the coach's methods, but rather one who recognizes and responds to the coach's efforts to meet her halfway. For a coachable coach, all players can be coachable athletes.

As adults, it is sometimes difficult to monitor our own level of adaptability. The key to staying coachable is making a personal commitment to ask ourselves, as each situation arises, "Exactly what is my agenda here?" A coachable coach will always return to her primary goal: to work with the temperament and abilities of the individual player to bring out that player's untapped power. We can't change other people, but by beginning with an honest appreciation for the qualities of the individual we can support each player to become her best.

The coachable coach asks permission to work with the player. She recognizes that it is a privilege, not a right, to enter into the child's personal space. When conflict arises, as it certainly will, the coachable coach steps back and asks the difficult questions about herself and her own reactions, rather than blaming the child for challenging her. By encouraging each player to be herself, to command herself, and to love herself, a coach can make an enormous contribution to each child's success.

• *Favoritism*

I talk to many parents of players at different levels of competition, particularly in soccer. Several have brought up the issue of "coach's pet." On some teams, every practice and every game seems to revolve around one particular player. In one case, the coach's pet, Sonia, was a very competent and skillful player who never attended practice. Her level of play, at that point in the season, was beyond that of her team-mates. I emphasize *at that point*, because that level will change—but, by then, it may be difficult to alter that player's attitude.

It's unfortunate that Sonia's coach allowed her to get away with this. Consider the message he is sending: one player is more important than the rest; the rules are different for each kid; and (sadly) it doesn't matter whether you come to practice or how hard you try, it only matters how "good" you are.

⊛   Every coach who has a child of his or her own on the team—and most youth coaches do—needs to be especially careful not to show favoritism or negativism to that child.

The coach's pet dynamic is interesting to watch, but it's also quite painful. Some team members will respond with open hostility towards the coach for showing favoritism. Others will want to know what's wrong with them, that they're not liked just as well. One parent told me, "My daughter's coach has certain ones he likes and certain ones he really doesn't like, and the other ones sort of fall in be-tween. I'm grateful my daughter is falling in between!"

Favoritism breeds distrust, hostility, fear, and anger. The team sees certain players getting special treatment and they try to figure out how they can get that kind of treatment. When a player focuses on trying to change herself just to please the coach, she is bound to be unsuccessful. This dy-namic is damaging not only to that player but to the coach's relationship with the entire team.

A "pet" system inevitably snowballs. Those who are well liked soon know it, and they begin to manipulate the system (skipping practices and getting away with it, for example). Their teammates begin to despise them, because it's safer to despise a peer than to be angry at an authority figure, particularly one you're trying hard to please.

The pet system also places pressure on the favored player because she doesn't know why she's being favored. More often than not, the favorites are players with the highest level skills, those who contribute in obvious ways to the team's scoring ability. Whatever it is they are doing, they have to make sure they keep doing it the same way or they risk losing "pet" status. They constantly fear making costly mistakes in play. And their peers' resentment becomes evident to them, making relationships uncomfortable. All this pressure can create hidden animosity between the favored player and the coach, since favoritism puts pressure on the pet to succeed and brings on the dislike of her teammates.

⊕   The idea that the person in charge will change the rules for individual players is a scary message, because every player wonders if the rules will change for her.

The pet system can also create hostility among the parents. In fact, this practice is like an insidious disease that infects the entire team.

How can we as coaches control the way we react to individual players? Fairness doesn't come automatically. Most of us need to work at maintaining a positive attitude and a sense of fair play.

There are two key elements in avoiding favoritism on the team. First, it's important for the coach to make an effort to appreciate the differences among individual team members. Each one brings something special to the team, and because they're all different, the coach gets twelve different experiences.

Coaches are human, however, and there will always be certain players who push your buttons. When that happens to me, I make an effort to appreciate that individual for affecting me in that way. The fact is, every time I've had a button pushed, it has given me an opportunity to reflect and learn from my own reaction. That is the second key element: the coach has to monitor his or her own reactions. If something you do or say is out of line, learn from that misstep. On days when I'm feeling taxed or stressed, it can be really hard to control my reactions. It has taken some very conscious coaching to ensure that I don't scapegoat certain players, and that I remain aware of what might be perceived as favoritism.

Ideally, we don't want to treat all kids identically, because they are all unique in their gifts. Some require more patience or affection or guidance than others. But their individual needs do not make them more or less likable. Giving each one the kind of attention she needs does not mean you are choosing favorites.

⚽   Being conscious of children's individual needs is an important step to treating them fairly. Most parents understand that fair treatment does not mean identical treatment.

As hard as coaches try, however, it may be impossible to feel equally fond of all the kids in our charge. That is where a basic fairness system comes in. Fairness means having a set of clear guidelines and sticking to them. For example, practices have specific beginning and ending times, and all players are expected to be there for that period of time. Similarly, coaches need clear rules regarding behavior— and the rules and the consequences need to be the same for every player.

⚽   If coaches make sure that the rules are the same for all players, and the consequences are the same, this will resolve a great deal of the "pet" problem.

I have a friend whose fifteen-year-old daughter Stephanie had been on a competitive soccer team since she was ten. She played the entire time with the same coach and the same group of girls, but she had a very unhappy experience that carried over into other areas of her life in damaging ways. Stephanie's coach was verbally abusive to her, condescending and belittling, and failed to give her a chance to play. She would be sent in the game for a minute or two to give somebody a break and then immediately called back out. In return for Stephanie's faithful practice attendance and her commitment to the team, that is how she was rewarded.

This negative experience affected her other sports. Stephanie was on her high school basketball team, and was a very good player. But every time she heard "Sub!" she would start walking off the basketball court without pausing to look up. She was so conditioned to being subbed, she automatically assumed the call was to her.

On many competitive teams, coaches play only those kids they consider the best players, and the others get very little opportunity to develop their game skills.

Another friend's daughter had a similar experience. Again, this was a girl who attended all practices. Jennifer was not a great soccer player, but she accompanied her team when it moved up from recreational to a competitive league. Her coach apparently decided that she wouldn't play. She literally sat on the bench for every game and never went in.

Jennifer's teammates became angry and resentful toward the coach because they felt she was being treated unfairly. Girls who were not attending practices but were better players played regularly in the games.

Ultimately, Jennifer quit the team, but she wouldn't go back to recreational soccer because it had been such an embittering experience. She wanted to stay with her teammates, and she decided that if she couldn't play with them she wasn't going to play at all. Fortunately, her parents allowed her to make the decision. It takes a great deal of self-respect to say, "I'm not going to be treated like this," and walk away.

• *Scapegoating*

A scapegoat is the opposite of coach's pet. Sometimes, there is one player who pushes all the wrong buttons. Instead of examining the feelings that are stirred up by this player, the coach may respond with anger, rejecting the kid and making her a scapegoat. In some cases, scapegoating becomes one of the "rules" of the team. The other players may become afraid that if they don't participate, they risk becoming the coach's scapegoat themselves.

It's impossible to be completely fair all the time. Some kids require more attention, and it can be exhausting. But when a coach's own emotions are in harmony, there's no way the players can stir them up. Something unresolved, however, can provide an emotional trigger—and some kids seem to have radar for your weak spots. When that happens, you must force yourself to look at the situation and determine why you reacted as you did. Without that kind of effort— without resolving it within yourself—you risk targeting that child as a scapegoat.

• *Dealing with the star player*

A related problem arises when you have one player who's scoring all the goals. That generally leads to the consensus that "this kid is the best player."

On my team, my best shooter was not my best player. My best shooter—the one who scored most of the goals— was a very good player. She was great on offense because she had fantastic peripheral vision. Since she was able to see the sides of the field, I usually played her as center. She was a great shooter and was able to get past some kids. She had pretty good footwork, although not the best on the team, and she had the speed to really move that ball down the field.

You might think this player, because she was a high scorer, would hog the ball. Just the opposite was true. She had the peripheral vision and she used it! It was great to watch her pass the ball around—that's a real strength. I have seen kids who are high scorers and have good footwork who decide they're going to play the game alone.

Naturally, everybody starts to see this great shooter as the best player on the team, so I have to work consistently at spotlighting the strengths of each player, pointing out that without a fantastic defense and midfielders this kid would not be able to score. She needs the entire team to help her. She needs to be able to get passes and she needs people to pass to.

⊕ On a team that works well together, there really is no such thing as a best player. Kids do tend to think that if one player scores most of the goals, she must be the best, but that's not the case. She has to rely on her team-mates to make it possible for her to score.

I once watched some of the girls on my soccer team playing a basketball game. They were all on the court—four of them from my soccer team, and one player I didn't know, Amy. Amy was clearly a natural basketball player. She would dribble the ball down the court and lay it up with great ease. But while she was a joy to watch, Amy was really also quite provocative. She would dribble the ball down, with four of her teammates yelling "Pass, pass, pass!"—and she wouldn't pass to anyone. I sat and watched her literally stand in one place, dribbling, with her teammates screaming, "I'm open! I'm open!" Everybody became stationary, the other team as well as her own team. She stood there for almost three minutes, just dribbling, trying to draw the other team to her so she could move in for the shot. She never considered passing the ball.

That's a coaching problem. I can tell you how I'd handle it, and it would be very simple. I once had the same problem with one of my soccer kids. "You're not passing that ball around," I told her, "so you can't stay in that position."

Since Amy is the center on her basketball team, she has the responsibility to create plays. Her job is to pass the ball around, to use her team members, to be able to see the court and know how to move around it, not by herself but with her team. If she can't do that, she shouldn't be in the position.

Since basketball is a team experience, Amy would have benefited from hearing her teammates talk about how they felt in a team meeting. The feedback would be great for her to hear, and it would be much better for her to hear it from her teammates than from her coach.

Now, when all that's done and Amy still doesn't change her actions, and the coach is not willing to remove her from the position, there is another way the coach could deal with the situation. She could instruct the teammates as follows: "Okay, from now on, when Amy gets the ball, just stop running. Let's let her dribble down the court and face five opponents and see how far she gets." When she sees that she is prevented from scoring—because five opponents are free to cover one girl—maybe she'll understand what it means to be a *team* player. That's a drastic move, but as I sat there watching that game I couldn't help thinking, "I'd do it in a heartbeat." Amy needed to hear it, she needed to see it, she needed to feel it.

Self-scrutiny

A friend of mine, the athletic director of a private school, talked with me about how she—like me, and every other coach I've known or witnessed—can get carried away, becoming angry with the kids, yelling and screaming at them in a way she never intended. This conversation led us to a realization: a key difference between the two of us and some other coaches we've known is that we force ourselves—and it's painful sometimes—to step back and observe our own behavior. We try to keep ourselves in check. We ask parents for feedback: "What do you think? Did I sound out of control? Was that inappropriate? Should I have handled it a different way?" We seek information. We recognize our fallibility as human beings.

Every time we ask ourselves a question about our coaching, we're becoming more conscious. The more conscious we become, the more caring—and the more effective— we are sure to be with the kids in our charge.

Most important, a conscious coach has to learn how to empower her players, rather than put them in a situation of powerlessness. This is a hard thing to do, since coaches have real authority and responsibility as well as (hopefully) some expert knowledge.

⚽ Coaches need to give direction to the players, but at the same time they need to place as much power as possible in the players' hands.

• *Overreacting*

One day I borrowed Debby's ball at practice. After I used it for the drill, I kicked it off to the side and we had our scrimmage. The ball disappeared, even though I was certain I had kicked it in the direction of all the other balls.

At the end of practice, missing her ball, Debby said several times, "The last time I saw it was when you kicked it over to the side. You were the last one to touch it, and then I didn't have it after that." Finally I exploded, "Okay, so you lost your ball. Your ball is missing and it's my fault, is that right? It's my fault. I'm to blame because you're missing your ball!" I was already at the end of my rope that day. "I didn't say it was your fault," Debby protested. "I don't want to deal with it right now, okay?" I told her, and I left.

Driving away, I was shaken by my reaction. How could I talk to a kid that way? It took only a few minutes of self-examination to come up with the answer—and it had absolutely nothing to do with soccer or this ten-year-old player.

At that time I was being prepared by my lawyer to testify in court about my assault, forced once again to relive the nightmare—forced to remember how I had failed to protect the employee who'd accompanied me, a young man who nearly lost his life. Going over that testimony was like focusing a spotlight on my error of judgment. I exploded at Debby because, at that moment, I simply couldn't handle feeling that something else was my fault—even the loss of a soccer ball!

I made it a point to talk to Debby privately before the next practice. I told her, "There was something else going on that upset me and I took it out on you. It was unfair and inappropriate and I'm sorry for it." Debby (just as forgiving as most ten-year olds) said, "It's okay. It's all right." I told her, "No, it's not all right." It's not all right, ever, for the kids to be mistreated. "It's not okay, but I can forgive you" is a very different response.

• *Apologizing*

My father and I were flying back from Chicago in his plane one day, when I was about fourteen years old. He was trying to make good time, so we were flying for quite a while at 11,000 feet, which is really pushing the oxygen level for a light plane. I happened to have some eucalyptus cough drops from my grandmother that I ate as candy. I was sucking on one when my father turned to me and said, "What the hell is that??" I was shocked at his uncharacteristically angry tone. "What's that smell? What are you eating?" "Some cough drops that Grandma gave me." "They smell awful!" he said. He seemed really upset, so I crunched it up and swallowed it.

A while later, after he had taken the plane to a lower altitude, my dad said, "I'm really sorry for snapping at you. You know, we were above 11,000 feet for a while, and I guess I was starting to feel the effects of the lack of oxygen. One of the effects is that you get irritable, and I took it out on you. I'm really sorry. I shouldn't have done that. I wasn't aware that I was pushing my limits."

What a great feeling that was for me! My dad always apologized when he said or did something hurtful. He gave me a tremendous gift by taking responsibility for his actions and apologizing for it when he knew I hadn't deserved it.

I was very proud, in my turn, when one of my team members told her mother (who passed the comment on to me) that I wasn't like her teacher at school because "when Kathy makes a mistake, she always says she's sorry." I wondered aloud why we adults have such difficulty accepting that we've made a mistake. The mother said, "Sometimes I think we'd rather go without food than apologize." An interesting analogy, I thought, because by not apologizing we are also going without food—food for the soul.

• *Observing and judging*

I make a practice of observing the bald eagles in a nearby national park. One day, as I watched, one of the young birds was frantically flapping its wings, trying to figure out how they worked. This year's bird, I noted, was much slower in development than the baby the year before, who was stronger overall.

It's interesting how we relate to nature—we're able to make observations without judgment. In nature, we *observe* behavior: a raccoon and a possum fighting, ducks protecting their babies, a snake hanging from a tree. Yet when we look at one another, we're judging all the time.

I'm certainly guilty of that. On the soccer team, I find

myself doing the same thing—looking at someone and wondering, "Why can't she kick harder? Why can't she do (x), (y), or (z)? How come she doesn't get this one simple step?" I'm judging players all the time. I'm becoming more aware of it and trying to change, trying to see these kids more as a part of nature that I can observe without judging. It shouldn't be so hard to observe them playing without attaching meaning to it, good or bad.

CHAPTER TWO
Communication

When I was an undergraduate social work student, I took a couples' counseling class. I was very struck by one of the professor's assertions. "The first thing you look for in a couple," he said, "is some type of communication. They may be screaming at each other, but they're still communicating. If a couple comes to you and there is no communication between them, the chances are they can't save the marriage. When the relationship has broken down so far they don't talk to one another, even about the little things, the marriage is probably over."

At the time, I thought that was a little extreme, yet I have referred back to that statement hundreds of times in the past fifteen years. In fact, it has inspired me many times to let someone know how I really feel about something they have said or done, because I believe it is necessary in order to maintain a thriving relationship with them. I painfully recall certain relationships in which I either did not have the courage to be honest about my feelings, or I felt I was not heard. These relationships do not thrive; they do not continue to grow and develop into more honest and trusting friendships.

Team Time

Early in my coaching I made a commitment to create an environment that encourages communication among players, coaches, and parents. The "team time" at the beginning and end of practices and games was a time when we all, players and coaches, could talk about anything that related to the team.

It was easy, however, to let the discussion jump all over the place as each person talked about what was on her mind—which could be anything at age ten! I made it a point to say "You're off task" or "Let's stay on task" every time someone started to digress from the topic of discussion. This way, they became so familiar with the rule they asked themselves before they spoke, "Is this related to what the team is talking about?" The players learned how to stay focused, but in order to do this they had to listen to what their teammates said.

I had one player who always had something to say, but it was often completely unrelated to what was being discussed by the team. At first I responded as I do with all the kids, stopping her midway through her question when I realized it wasn't related. This particular child, however, was not intending to disrupt the discussion. She seemed to have an unusually high level of anxiety, and had difficulty refraining from saying whatever was on her mind. With her, I needed to use a different approach. Before calling on her, I began asking, "Susan, we're talking about —— right now. Is what you have to say related to that?" Frequently she would answer, "Not really," and I'd go on to ask for other contributions to our topic.

After a few meetings, I no longer needed to ask Susan if her comment was related. She would raise her hand and say, "This is related to what we're talking about," and then offer the team her valuable insights and ideas. There were also times when, even after being given her opportunity to speak, Susan would smile and say, "This isn't really related," and stop herself!

The team time was, without a doubt, one of the most valuable means of developing the team. The girls knew the time was always going to be there, and they came to depend on it. Some of them came to practice with an issue they wished to bring up to their teammates. On these occasions, we were hardly in our semi-circle when they threw their hands up, begging, "I have something to say to the team! Please, I have something to say to the team!" These are exactly the words I used when I was about to address the team.

• *Teamwork works*

By the end of our first season together, everyone commented on how well the team was passing. One coach told me we were by far the best passing team they had ever played. The girls were working well together on the field—even though, in the beginning, I couldn't get them to pass to save their lives! They'd been almost rebellious about it. In fact, I took Lynn out of offense and put her on defense because she wouldn't pass the ball (though she complained that the others weren't passing to her).

The previous season, according to parents' reports, there were one or two players that were simply never passed to, and there were pairs (or threes) who would always give one another the ball. This is far from unusual. I know of very competitive high school teams that have the same problems with passing the ball.

The improvement in the team's passing ability was not primarily a matter of technical skill—we hadn't focused particularly on learning to pass the ball. I believe that our team meetings were as important to the team's improvement as the actual practice.

Girls that age tend to see the ball as another element in the friendships and alliances on which they focus so much attention. To put it bluntly, they only pass to their friends. The great accomplishment of the team meetings was getting the girls to acknowledge each other as teammates, even when they were not close friends. This gave them a different (and more mature) perspective on what they were doing when they were passing the ball.

Later in the season, the girls would bring the ball down the field—near enough to the goal to attempt to score—and pass it off to another player who put it in. They got as much of a thrill if their teammate scored and they'd assisted.

• *Team meetings*

When I was a kid and misbehaved, my mother would say, "Everything you do reflects on your parents, so when you do something bad, that makes us look bad." I used to scream back, "*I'm* responsible for my actions. Everything I do reflects only on *me*. It has nothing to do with you."

Now I realize she had a point. As a coach, what your team does, on the field and off the field, reflects on you. It reflects whether you have taken the time to point out good sportsmanship and discuss situations of bad communication, questionable behavior, and unfair treatment, as they have come up. The coach is in charge of the team's culture.

⚽ How the girls talk to one another, how they deal with their opponents, how they talk about the other team, how they handle the high-fives at the end of each game—everything the players do reflects on the coach.

Every issue that comes up should be discussed with the team, all together, in a setting where everyone has a chance to say how she feels. This is a "debriefing." Instead of telling the team what I wanted ("briefing" them), I listened to how they felt about a situation. Even if this took fifteen minutes of practice time, it was generally a more valuable use of fifteen minutes than the drill I was planning to do.

⚽ "Team time" needs to be programmed into the schedule. Every practice began with the team coming together, even if there was nothing particular to discuss. At the end of practices, the team came together to hear announcements and be dismissed. The players also came together before every game as well as at halftime, and they checked in with the coach after the game, before leaving the field.

Our recreational team practices lasted an hour and fifteen minutes, twice a week, and we usually began practice with a team meeting. At team meetings all the players sat in a semi-circle, without water bottles or other distractions, and simply listened to each other.

A coach's corrections and the team discussion of a situation need to come as soon as possible after a problem has arisen. It's no different than a parent or teacher disciplining a child. You don't discipline her a month later for skipping school, or hours later for hitting her little brother. You've got to do it at the time it happens.

Any problem should be brought up at the very next meeting. Don't wait two weeks and then say, "A couple of weeks ago . . ." It's gone. It's done. It's over with! Make use of a situation when it happens.

• *Managing meetings*

It would be revealing to take a snapshot of a team as the members sit down together. I once observed a coach gathering his team to discuss something at the end of their practice. As they sat down, one girl had her back to another; one was hidden behind a couple of other girls. They weren't even all facing the coach. They stayed this way throughout his entire speech.

The simplest thing you can do to manage the group process is have the team begin each practice sitting in a semi-circle facing the coach. No one is allowed to sit behind someone else, and no one can sit "next to" the coach. The coaches also sit, putting everybody at the same level.

Listening skills are crucial. The rule is, "When I'm talking, you're listening, you're not talking. When you're talking, I'm listening, I'm not talking. One person speaks at a time, and we give 100 percent attention to that speaker." It takes constant reminders, but it works!

I have always made a point of using team-conscious language, such as, "I have something to say to the team" and "Please pay attention to your teammates." I allowed each person a chance to speak, even at the risk of spending too much time in the meeting. But if someone began to make comments unrelated to the discussion, I cut her off, saying, "That's not what we're talking about now. Does someone have something to say on this topic?"

After each person spoke, I summed up, repeating what the player said. Sometimes it became clear that I'd misheard them. I'd say, "So what you just said is . . ." and the speaker would say, "Well, no, what I meant was . . ." Then I summed up again. It worked beautifully to let them know they'd been heard.

⊕   The five basic rules of a team meeting are:
    1. The team sits in a semi-circle facing the coach.
    2. One person speaks at a time and is listened to.
    3. The group is a team, and our choice of words reflects that.
    4. Everyone gets to speak, but every contribution must be on the topic being discussed (unless it's appropriate to raise a new topic).
    5. The coach acts as facilitator, maintaining order and summing up what each person has said.

It was wonderful to observe the girls' participation in our meetings. They became great speakers and fantastic, respectful listeners. No one interrupted or disrupted the group, or got fidgety. Anyone observing our team meetings would have been astounded by the attentiveness of those ten-year olds and by the wisdom behind their eyes. What's more, I noticed that I'd become a better listener too.

How it works

• *A sample debriefing: practice captains*

We started having two practice captains, on a rotating basis, at each of our two weekly practices (see chapter five). I was surprised at how well it worked, but I was not really surprised at what it stirred up among the team members.

I purposely held off on debriefing for the first two practices. I thought it would be useful for the girls to hold onto their feelings without any guidance from their coaches. But some careful discussion was clearly necessary. Intense emotions had been stirred up, which could be productive to the team's development only if they were discussed openly and honestly, with a respectful hearing.

The coach's job in the debriefing is to facilitate, simply by allowing the practice captains and their teammates to talk about their group dynamics. There are several important steps the coach can take to manage this job. First, she should make sure there is enough time allotted to the meeting to allow each girl to be heard completely. Second, the coach must require that every girl listen attentively to her teammates. Third, the coach can be particularly helpful in summing up and repeating what each child has said, perhaps in the form of a question. This serves several purposes: the speaker sees that the coach felt her contribution was worthwhile; the group has the salient points emphasized; and the speaker has further opportunity to clarify what she meant.

As adults we often make the mistake of thinking that every opinion a child offers needs to be given either our approval or our disapproval. I have observed this in myself as well as in other adults. We hear something from a child and we rush in to agree or disagree, erroneously assuming that our opinion counts more than theirs. I have to remind myself frequently that my job in debriefings is to listen. Only after hearing all the opinions should I give my own assessment. In many cases, my role is simply to sum up conflicting opinions. These conflicting opinions do not have to be changed or corrected; often, there is nothing to be resolved. They merely need to be expressed and heard.

The most important attribute of a good facilitator, for any group, is genuine concern with the group's development. A facilitator understands that tension exists and she is comfortable permitting it to take its course, once all group members have been heard. The facilitator has confidence that the group's members can resolve conflict on their own. She realizes that a rush toward resolution will certainly deprive the members of the opportunity to work through their difficulties, once they recognize the problems exist.

As the facilitating coach, I first asked how the four practice captains felt about their roles. They all agreed it was difficult to get their teammates to take them seriously. They talked about the frustration of trying to organize their drill teams in order to be able to proceed with practice. They found it especially hard, they said, to tell their friends to be quiet.

There was considerable anger and frustration between the practice captains and their teammates. Mary seemed about to burst. She had her arm extended rigidly high above her head and was hopping up and down on the balls of her feet, trying to get me to call on her. "Please, please, I have something to say about the practice captains. I have something to say about the practice captains!" she pleaded, hardly able to contain herself.

Finally Mary got her turn and said, "Well, some of the practice captains are sort of bossy to us and they're saying things like, 'Well, you better do this because *I'm* the practice captain.'" "So it feels like they're bossing you around," I said. "Yeah, and they're like, 'I'm going first because *I'm* the practice captain,'" she added.

Immediately, her practice captain, Liz, shot her arm up and said, "Well, sometimes it's hard to get everyone to get in line because they're all fighting about who's going to go first, so I said, 'Well, I'm the practice captain, so maybe I should go first.'" "So it's hard to get your drill teams to organize, and you think if you go first they'll eventually line up," I said. "Yeah, otherwise they just keep fighting." "Well," retorted Mary, "you don't have to be so bossy about it and say, like, 'I'm the practice captain so I'm going first!'"

I summarized, "So Mary is saying that there is a way of saying something without being bossy." Liz shot back, "Well, with *some* people it doesn't matter how you say it, they're still going to think you're being bossy." "That's a good point," I said. "Some people will have difficulty with everything you say, and it's just plain difficult for them to be told what to do. And there are certainly ways of communicating, like Mary is suggesting, that will not be authoritarian or bossy. That's difficult for anyone, adult or child, to do. There's no easy way to figure it out. You sort of have to try different things and see what works."

"Does anyone have any ideas," I asked, "about how we might better communicate with our teammates?" One player offered, "We could say, come on you guys, let's be quiet or we're going to lose our practice time." "So pointing out what you all lose might be useful?" I asked. "Yeah," someone else said, "if we just say something like, 'We have to be quiet now,' then it's to the whole team [and not to any particular girl]." "Well," I said, "those are some good ideas. I don't think there are any easy answers, but it's important for us to talk about it as we go along so that we all know how each other feels. You want to keep having practice captains?" I asked. "Yeah!" was the enthusiastic reply from all of them.

• *Coaching from the sidelines*

Martina came up with a really good point in one of our team meetings after she had gone to several college women's soccer games: "Maybe instead of you telling us what to do, we should be talking more on the field."

Isn't that beautiful?!

Obviously, the players are going to hear one another better than they can hear any of us from the sidelines, and they know what they're going to do. Martina could say to a team member, "Go left," and that person's going to start to do that—even though the coaches might be telling her to go right. By coaching from the sidelines, we are just messing up their plans!

Martina went on to explain that "all of us need to start talking more, we need to start telling each other what we're going to do and what the other should do. That way," she said, "the coaches won't have to say anything because we'll be doing it, and we *should* be the ones doing it."

Toward the end of the first season it was obvious the girls had really learned to pass and to work as a team. That took a great deal of work, not just on communication and ball skills, but also on all the counterproductive behaviors and the conflicts among the players.

At a team meeting, Dave asked how the members felt about their parents' and coaches' behavior on the sidelines during games. Were we yelling too much? Were we giving too many instructions? What would they like to see change? Their opinions were unanimous: it was okay to cheer, but they would rather we did not use names of individual players. They also asked that we keep instructions to an absolute minimum—and these should come only from coaches, not from parents. But, they said, the coaches also needed to say less because we were confusing and distracting them. Parents should stick to cheering, and then only after a particular play: "Good hustle," "Nice pass, Blue!" "Way to go,

Blue!" Cheers should be general—no names, please!

Dave and I followed up the meeting with a letter to the parents. Before the next game we gathered players and parents together so that we could relay the team's sentiments to the parents, in the presence of team members.

- *Sharing power within the team*

The girls voiced objection to our "yelling" at them during games, and I asked them to help keep us in check by pointing out when we were yelling—even if they had to leave the sub box (see chapter five) to talk to us.

Not long after this discussion, early in one game, I was shouting instructions from the sidelines. "Go! Go! Move!" Mary, standing on the sidelines beside me, turned and said, "Kaaathyy . . ." "What?" I just glanced at her and turned back to the field, and went back to screaming, "Go, go, go!"

Mary said again, "*Kaaathy*, you said you weren't going to *dooo* that." "Do what? Do what?" I was half listening to her and half watching the game. "You said you weren't going to yell any more." Her mom intervened, "Wait a minute, Kathy's not yelling. She's telling them what to do." Mary just shook her head. I said to Mary, "Does it sound like I'm yelling?" "Yeah." "You're right. And I asked you to make sure you tell me if I'm yelling. Thanks, Mary."

Mary's reminder made me realize I had become frustrated because a player was not in position, and there was some anger in my voice. I was yelling *at* them rather than *to* them. Mary called me on it, God love her.

This is an example of what may be the most important thing about the team experience: coaches learning how to give their kids a sense of being power*ful* rather than power*less*.

Confidentiality

I make a conscious effort to use respectful, caring language—of course, that is not to say I always succeed. I make big mistakes, but I work hard to not make the same mistake twice. This hasn't been that difficult, because the errors I've made have caused such emotional pain to the child (and to me) that I never want to commit the offense again.

I think one of my biggest mistakes was an act that betrayed the team's trust in the safe boundaries they had come to rely on during team time. This betrayal of trust was unfortunately at the expense of one child in particular.

Carla was frustrated at one game because I had put the girls in unfamiliar positions to slow our game so we wouldn't run up the score. As she is a very strong offensive player, I put her on defense. Like all kids, she wanted to score a goal. She was angry about my decision and made a point of showing it.

Her teammates were annoyed that she was behaving that way—especially those who had been "stuck" on defense the whole season. Carla, unable to contain her frustration, announced to her teammates—though not to me—that she was quitting the team.

This information didn't reach me until just before our next practice. I overheard some of the other girls talking about Carla quitting the team, and a few of the parents mentioned it as well. I was taken completely by surprise.

When one of the players has confided in me—about anything—I keep it confidential. I may see the value of bringing certain concerns up before the team, but if the child doesn't want me to, I keep it between the two of us. Eventually she will either raise the issue during team time or ask me to bring it up. In this particular case, however, the information had been loosely thrown around, first to several teammates, then from teammates to parents, and finally to coaches.

Since the information appeared to be public knowledge, I decided to raise the topic during our team time. It completely blind-sided Carla when I asked her, in front of the team, if she was planning to quit. I watched her scan the entire group with great unease and I knew that I had stepped over that protective boundary we had developed as a team. Carla quickly denied threatening to quit, and I tried to do a little damage control. I talked about having such passion to play the game that it's hard to handle upsets (such as having to play unfamiliar positions). The damage was done, however. I left practice that day wondering what would cause me to put Carla on the spot in a way that was sure to hurt her.

That evening, I received a call from Carla's dad, who was understandably upset. While he understood, he said, that his daughter could use a lesson in sportsmanship, embarrassing her in front of the team was not the way to do it. I had to agree with him. He correctly argued that I should have talked to Carla privately to find out what issues had been behind the threat to quit, and only then talked to the team. I felt this criticism so deeply, I knew it would take some serious reflection to understand my own actions.

Carla had confided in others about something that concerned me and I felt betrayed by her. This poked at my ego, and I, in turn, chose a course of action that would betray her confidence in front of the team. For a few days following the incident, I remained angry at this child for creating the situation that caused me to respond the way I did. Then I realized I had to take responsibility for my behavior—which made me even angrier! I needed to forgive Carla for striking out at me with her statement about quitting and forgive myself for reacting the way I did.

Carla and I talked privately about the situation at the next practice and I was happy we could return to the game as teammates.

Verbal cues
- *"Edit"*

During my first season as coach, I kept things very simple. I could see that the kids were not yet functioning as a team. I had to keep them focused and get through the fundamentals of passing and dribbling. We worked really hard, and it paid off. By the end of the season, we were far better in basic skills than the teams we played.

During the second season, I began to introduce more difficult moves. Inevitably, I found, someone would start goofing around or asking questions just to distract the others, and the whole team would get off task. The constant interruptions were frustrating.

The problem was solved when we introduced "editing" as a technique for making players more conscious of their behavior and its effect on the team. After spending several practice times teaching fakes, changes of direction, and other important dribbling skills, Susan asked, "Is any of this really going to help us in a game?" I immediately shot back, "No, Susan, none of this is going to help you in a game."

It was immediately clear that I had overreacted to Susan's straightforward question about the drills, and at the next practice, during our team meeting, I made a point of apologizing to the team. I also pointed out the reasons for my frustration. "Because of all the questions that distract from what I'm trying to share, I begin thinking that everything one of you says is just something else to get us off task. So, when Susan asked that question, I jumped on her! And yet, it was a great question. If I had taken it seriously," I explained, "I would have been able to show you right then how to use that skill in a game. Instead I got angry and put her down, and I disrespected the entire team in the process.

"But I'm also aware that a small number of you are playing games with me. It doesn't matter how many times I go over something, you continue to ask questions about the same point. As soon as I get two words out—'Okay, now we're going to'—before I can even say what we're going to do, one or two of you will say, 'But I don't get it!' How could you 'get it' when I haven't even gotten to the point? From now on," I said very deliberately, "when I'm trying to teach a drill, any time you start to say something, **count to ten**. When you get to ten, **edit** whatever it is you want to say. You'll often find that what you were going to say was something that would take time away from the team. If there is anything left to say after you've edited, then by all means share it with us. But make sure it's something that will contribute to this soccer team. Remember, count to ten, edit, and get back to us."

After that, for the next two practices—and that's all it took—as soon as someone began to interrupt, I would turn to her and say, "Count to ten right now, edit, get back to me," and I'd walk away to teach whatever I was going to teach. Another one would say, "But I don't get it!" "Count to ten, edit, get back to me."

⚽ As with the other "cues" discussed in this chapter, it's essential to have a short verbal reminder to use every time these situations arise. It is a way for the coach and player to shift the focus from the child to the behavior that needs to change. (This is a coaching shortcut, but it is also a token that the players and coach are working together to get the job done.)

The problem of interruptions was almost completely solved, simply by making the girls more conscious of their disruptive behavior through "editing."

• *"Do your best"*
    I had a couple of girls who would say at the beginning of every new drill, "I can't do it. I can't do it!" At first, I ex-

plained over and over again, but they would simply stand there shaking their heads, repeating, "I can't do it." Gradually I realized this was a plea for individual attention. Once I recognized the problem, I changed my approach.

⚽ It's important to let the players know directly when a change is going to be made. Otherwise, a lot of time and energy will be wasted as they resist the change. It's also important to give the reasons for a change, so it doesn't appear they are being punished.

In the next team meeting I gave a little speech: "I know that some of these skills are hard, and some of you keep telling me you can't get it. I've been trying to give one-on-one attention for those who can't get it, but that's going to stop today. From now on, if you tell me you can't follow a skill I'm trying to teach, I will just say to you, 'Do the best you can'—because eventually you will get it. If it's a new skill, I'll show you once again. My giving individual attention takes away too much from the team. I'm not angry with you, but I want you to know there will be this change. You just do your best. That's good enough for me, and it's good enough for your teammates."

From that point, as soon as the two started saying, "I can't get it," I'd just say, "Do your best" and turn away. Turning away became a coaching tactic, giving the girls responsibility for doing their best. And they accepted that responsibility. The kids stopped calling for help unnecessarily.

• *The "Panic Pass"*

I'm sure I'm not the only coach with players suffering from the "panic pass" syndrome (receiving the ball and kicking it without even looking up—often to an opposing player), but I'm probably one of the few coaches who also plays on a soccer team and suffers the syndrome in her own game.

At the start of a game most athletes feel some anxiety, which can actually enhance performance, if it is not too severe. It takes me ten to fifteen minutes to settle into playing a solid game, which means ten or fifteen minutes of "panic passing."

All players make their share of panic passes, but most gain some control over it with experience. They become *desensitized* to receiving the ball, so it no longer induces a panicked reaction. Some players, however, become *sensitized* instead, and the panic reaction continues or worsens.

Diane made tremendous progress in getting over her panic reaction, with just a little help from me. She was an enthusiastic player, fearless in spite of her small size. She aggressively attacked the ball, undaunted by the size or number of her opponents. I found her truly inspiring to watch (especially since I have trouble myself keeping an aggressive attitude against larger players). Nevertheless, it was extremely frustrating at the beginning of the season to see that wonderful energy go to waste, when, on winning the ball, Diane invariably lost possession with a panic pass.

For the first several weeks, Dave and I wasted our breath on absolutely useless instructions: "Diane, look first. Don't just kick the ball!" "Gain control of the ball, then pass to someone." "Look up! Find someone to pass to first!" We were going to ruin this kid's confidence if we couldn't find a way to help her work on managing the anxiety she felt. This was one of the many times I prayed for a way to help one of the girls and got an immediate answer.

I told the team that "Receive" and "Scan" would be the new approach to coaching this problem, and I expected all players to say to themselves, "Receive," when they gained possession of the ball, and then "Scan" while looking to see who was open for a pass or where they might carry the ball. Then I spoke to Diane individually and told her I was going to try my best to help her with this, so we could improve her game and take advantage of all her energy. Diane is one of the most coachable kids I've ever worked with. She was willing to try anything I suggested, which, ironically, may have been part of the problem. Diane was so eager to do a great job on the field she was mentally jumping ahead. With the new approach, she would be coached simply to receive, then scan. We completely eliminated all other instruction.

This approach was difficult for the team to adjust to, and nearly impossible for Diane. I began to wonder whether I had misheard my answer to prayer. After several practices, though, I began to see Diane saying to herself as the ball approached, "Receive," and then, once she had the ball, "Scan." The entire team reaped the benefits of her discipline. In a game late that season, Diane received the ball close to our twenty-yard line. She scanned the field, found a receiver, and made a perfect pass that resulted in a goal! I walked down to our smallest fullback and said, "Diane, that goal started with you. Good job!" She gave me a huge smile and nodded in agreement.

• *"Do a body scan"*

There was another player on the team who ended up in tears at nearly every practice and game. My first season with Heather, I offered a little TLC (tender, loving care) every time she fell or was run into or was hit by the ball. After going through an entire season, however, with no change in the pattern of behavior, I realized my response was probably doing her a disservice. Ideally, children grow towards learning how to take care of themselves—occasionally revisiting the old ways that once worked. But if their immature behavior continues to bring rewards with influential people such as teachers, parents, and coaches, the behavior becomes harder to change.

In Heather's case, I stopped paying attention to the aches, pains, bruises, and tears. I didn't ignore her, I just stopped attending to her pleas. As soon as the tears began, whether in a game or practice, I simply pulled her out. During games, however, this became disruptive, since I had to pull her out every few minutes. Her teammates were at a disadvantage because they never knew who was working with them. They'd get used to the sub and then Heather would be ready to go in again.

Without singling out Heather, I brought up the issue of injury in a team meeting. I explained that it was desensitizing to a coach when there were repeated tears with no physical ailment, and constantly pulling a player from the game was extremely disruptive to team play. "Next time you wipe out, in a game or at practice," I told them, "do a quick body scan. Ask yourself, 'Do I have a real physical pain?' If not, what should you do?" Most responded, "Get up and keep playing!"

At the next day's game, Heather took the hardest fall I had seen her take. She winced and looked as if she would cry, then stopped, jumped up, and took off after the ball. It was remarkable to witness. After the game I went to her and said, "You played the best soccer I've ever seen you play. You were fantastic today!" "Yeah," she said, "and I even fell really hard. At first I thought I was hurt, but then I said, 'No, I'm not hurt,' and I just got up and ran!" In my view, whatever else happened that season, this single success was more reward than any coach could hope for.

During practice one day, Shari wiped out. She took a nasty fall and began crying. Dave and I both ran over to her. She was unable to make eye contact and couldn't be specific about what was hurting. I suggested it might be her ribs, because of how she fell. She went along with this, but couldn't describe the specific pain.

Shari remained on the field propped up on one arm, neither sitting nor lying down, a position I judged would be impossible with a fractured rib. She punched the ground with her fist, facing down, still avoiding eye contact. Although she stopped crying pretty quickly, she insisted she could not get up. In the time we waited for her mom to arrive to pick her up, the arm she had used to support herself became the arm that hurt (and from the way she was propped up on it, that didn't surprise me).

Needless to say, this injury took valuable time away from practice, as we tried to assess the situation. After about twenty minutes, Shari let us take her off the field so we could continue to practice. As soon as her mom arrived Shari began wailing, but within a few minutes she was ready to practice again.

At the following practice, the same thing happened. Shari wiped out during a drill and said she couldn't get up—again, avoiding eye contact with anyone. Suddenly it dawned on me: she's not hurt physically; she is suffering from a debilitating case of humiliation. Unlike Heather, Shari wasn't looking for attention. She was paralyzed with embarassment at wiping out.

This time I knew not to ask Shari if she could move off the field. Instead I told her to get off the field—not because I was angry with her, but because I felt that was the best way to help her resolve her embarrassment and overcome her problem. Our practice continued for another thirty minutes while Shari remained on the sidelines, head down, jabbing a stick into the ground.

This was another kid who needed a little help in transcending a debilitating pattern of behavior.

I rounded up balls while Dave was organizing a scrimmage. Putting balls in the bag, I asked Shari—without looking at her, since she was still avoiding eye contact—"Are you still hurting, Shari?" "Um!" she grunted and jabbed the ground harder with her stick. "Is it a body hurt or a pain in your heart?" I asked, continuing to put the equipment away. "I don't know!" she almost shouted. "Yeah, it's sort of hard to figure it out, because they both hurt, but in different ways," I began. "A body hurt is when you can feel your bones or muscles actually aching, and a pain in the heart is when you're sad or maybe embarrassed. Sometimes I get that pain in my heart when I've wiped out in front of a bunch of people. It's like I feel so stupid because they all saw me and they might be laughing at me. You saw that in the scrimmage, when Lisa tripped me and I went flying." Shari looked up at me and giggled. "I checked quickly to see if I was hurt physically, and when I realized I wasn't, I jumped up and got back in the game. I was really embarrassed, but I knew if I stayed down, everyone would focus on me. This way works pretty well for me, and I'm someone who has wiped out a million times in front of people. I've got major experience in this area, Shari!" Again she looked at me and giggled. I then gave Shari my best advice.

☻   When you take a fall, do a quick body scan. If there's no pain in your muscles or bones, jump up and move on.

"What do you think about trying that, just to see?" "O.K.," she smiled and shrugged her shoulders. Soon after, Shari was back on the field.

Her mom had been standing behind us the whole time this conversation was going on. "Kathy, you know her so well," she said, "sometimes I think you are Shari!" The funny thing is, I am very much like her daughter—the stubbornness and the anger at wiping out, whether physically or emotionally. Like Shari, I am very hard to reach during those times. But this toughness on myself can also be an asset.

However, personalities like Shari's and mine need gentle guidance from truly caring people, so that we may make positive use of our toughness. Otherwise we run the risk of getting stuck in a pattern of self-reproach that leads to self-defeat.

CHAPTER THREE
Physical Conditioning

Times have changed

I was talking with my brother, Paul, about how, when we were kids, learning sports skills was a matter of trial and error—on our own. When my sister and I dribbled a soccer ball down the field, it was hard work for anyone to get it away from us. We were not unusual. We played street ball all the time—soccer, football, or kickball—with the neighborhood kids.

Paul and I wondered why it's such a challenge to teach skills to young players. The problem is not with one or two of the kids—the whole team needs step-by-step instruction.

When the players on my team began running laps, they could hardly make it once around the field, which I found amazing. Children's lives are different now. They play computer games. There are usually not as many kids in a neighborhood, because families are smaller. And parents supervise their children more closely because of the fear of crime.

When my brothers and sisters and I came home from school, our mother wouldn't hear from us until dinner time—and then she had to go outside and ring a bell. Around dinner time we'd start to listen. "Hey, that's the Donovans' bell," someone would say. "No, that's the Williams' bell." The house up the street had one kind of bell and we had another, and the two mothers would come out their front doors and ring their bells, while other parents whistled or yelled for their children to come in. At one time I think there were forty kids on my street. We were never home because we were outside playing.

Today, who would want their ten-year-old girl out running around in the streets, playing games with God knows who? And, there wouldn't be enough kids for a game now, because they all have different activities after school. In the summer, if the parents are both working, the kids are at camp. At camp, instead of playing ball games, they're involved in crafts and theatre or water activities, or learning camping skills. These are great activities, but they don't involve ball skills or playing field skills. If the kids go to a sports camp, they get to play ball for only a two-week period instead of every day of the year, as we did.

So we get players on our teams who have never played with a ball. They haven't developed that kind of coordination. And they've missed out on the strategy and tactics, as well as the excitement, of dealing with a group or a team. They have not had the experience of initiating an activity and organizing their friends to participate with them. By missing out on the group-play experience, they have also missed a terrific opportunity to develop problem-solving skills—one of the most important of all life skills. In the classroom, on the playground at recess, in all their organized after-school activities, an adult is usually there to facilitate problem-solving, to set rules and enforce them. The activities of most kids today are structured by parents, teachers, and coaches.

- *Running laps*

Physical conditioning at this age is important. Many people (including some coaching experts) think that ten-year olds don't need to run laps. I think they do need to run laps—for conditioning, never for punishment. Our recreational soccer team did five minutes of running for the first two or three practices—after the first practice, that is, when they barely made it around the field one time! They were really slow, breathing in gasps, hyperventilating, cramping, experiencing stitches in their sides from the tension in their shoulders. This was a foreign experience to them.

I made them do it anyway. The first time we did it, I let them run any way they liked. At the next practice, I said, "Today I want you to breathe in through your noses and out through your mouths." When they did, it slowed their breathing. They were surprised to realize they were able to run farther and longer.

At the third practice, I had them try correct nostril breathing. "Now I want you to breathe in through your nose and out through your nose, so that you never open your mouth. It's all through the nose. It's going to feel really tough at first, but try to do it anyway, and stay conscious of your breathing. And if you do lapse into mouth breathing, observe how you feel." Somebody asked, "Why do we have to breathe this way? It's too hard!" "If you can keep your breathing under control, you'll be able to perform better," I told them. "You'll be able to run longer, because your muscles are going to get the right kind of fuel. I'm telling you to do this because I know from experience, as an athlete, how important breathing is." They started practicing it conscientiously.

At that point, we were still doing our standard five minutes of running laps. Then Dave pointed out, "This isn't going to do much good unless we keep increasing the time." So we went to six minutes, then seven minutes, then eight minutes. The girls were actually doing better, but they didn't realize it. Then one day Dave had them do five minutes of running laps followed by another five minutes of a running exercise, using a square formation. At the end he asked, "How do you feel?" Everyone said, "That was fun!" Dave told them, "You know, you just ran ten minutes straight. The only difference was that the first five minutes were spent running around the field and the other five playing this game. But it's all running! You did the running and no one is complaining or out of breath." That was a really smart approach.

Dave has done a number of running drills, to keep the

running fun and keep them motivated. The problem with the drills is that it's not continuous running—the players have to wait for their turn—and there's no way for them to measure their progress, as in running laps. We decided to use a combination of running games, relay races, and running laps.

One day, when the players were supposed to do nine minutes of laps, both Dave and I forgot to stop them, and the girls did eleven minutes of straight running! Every one of them did very well, even the ones who complained most in the beginning. My biggest complainer had even volunteered to be the pace setter that time (covered later in this chapter). These kids ended eleven minutes of running not even breathing hard. In fact, their breathing was so regulated, you could hardly tell they had run at all. It was magnificent.

Toward the end of the season we changed to running laps with the ball, which gave them an additional focus during the running as well as additional practice with ball skills. This approach worked the best. The complaining virtually disappeared.

When I assisted at my brother-in-law's practice, I watched his fifth-graders running laps around the field. Except for one girl, the players were in terrible shape and it was clearly a matter of conditioning. The one athlete, who was fast and had a good stride, was always in the lead. The others took one lap around the field trying to keep up with her. When they couldn't, they just dropped out and started walking.

The team's conditioning and endurance helped us in games when we didn't have enough players to provide adequate subs. I could see it working, particularly in comparison to other teams we played.

• *Mind and body*

I could tell that the girls were seeing and feeling their own physical progress, but I felt it would be helpful for me to draw their attention to it a little more. I began to say to them, as they came off the field, "How are you feeling? You feeling strong? How's the breathing?" I wanted them to report on what they were feeling as a way of keeping them tuned in to their bodies. The goal was to get them to the point where they were just *being* while running, conscious only of their physical selves. Staying mindful brings the runner into a meditative state and takes the effort out of running laps.

For some people, breathing control seems to come naturally. I noticed Susan as the girls were running laps one day. There was no effort at all in her running as she made her way around the field. Her breathing was beautifully regulated.

The words I use in instructing the soccer team encourage me in my personal physical conditioning. As I go out on my own runs, I hear myself saying to the team, "There's no point to running unless you step it up and keep doing a little more each time." And when I begin to think the status quo is good enough, I realize if I don't practice what I preach I'd better not be preaching it!

• Styles in running

I've noticed there are a few players on the team who can pace themselves so they finish the run without stopping. This is primarily a matter of psychology. Most kids go full speed and then stop, full speed again and stop. In spite of all the reminders to slow down the pace, they'll keep running until they have to stop.

There are also players who stop running when they are passed by another runner or two. They don't have the emotional strength to say, "That's all right, I'm not in the lead, but this is where I am."

• The pace setter

When it's time to run laps, one of the girls is assigned, on a rotating basis, the job of setting the pace for the run.

The pace setter maintains a speed that no one is allowed to exceed. By keeping a steady, manageable pace, the girls can develop real endurance.

Before I introduced this system, the laps turned into a race. By the time the players made it to the end of the field, they were exhausted. The pace setting was a great solution. It allowed the girls to appreciate their own pace, instead of comparing themselves to their teammates. Also, they learned to appreciate the responsibility of doing a job and doing it right.

⊛   The team was told they couldn't pass the pace setter, or even come within ten feet of her. In the beginning, the coach might choose the slowest player in the beginning to serve as pace setter. Putting her in that position keeps her running because she has a job to do. And since no one can pass her, there's no pressure on her.

It worked out beautifully. For the most part, they all kept running. They sometimes dropped out for a while, but usually they got back in. My brother-in-law also reported great success using this approach with his team.

• *The breathing captain*

No serious runner breathes in and out through the mouth. Probably most runners breathe in through the nose and out through the mouth, but to slow their breathing even more, they breathe in through the nose and out through the nose. Nostril breathing worked wonders for our team. The girls reported significant changes: they felt stronger, they didn't hyperventilate, they didn't get as tired. The correct breathing enabled the players to get the conditioning that kept them strong in games.

When I first tried to get the girls to work on their breathing, I'd hear the usual "I can't do it" or "It doesn't work."

But I kept bringing their attention back to the breathing. Each time I said, "Watch your breathing," they would shut their mouths and breathe through their noses. They soon started to feel the difference.

Eventually, we had two lap-running jobs: the pace setter and the breathing captain who called attention to the breathing. When I first came up with the idea of a breathing captain, I thought nobody would volunteer, but in fact there was always a little skirmish over who was going to do it.

This method worked really well. We'd hear the breathing captain call out to the team every now and then, "Watch your breathing." That's all the players needed to become more conscious of it. Either they were made aware they weren't breathing correctly, and closed their mouths and started breathing right, or they were already breathing correctly and the reminder drew their attention to it.

⚽   Performance monitoring is more effective when it comes from peers rather than a coach. It's also a way to encourage the players to coach one another, whether they're playing or running laps.

CHAPTER FOUR
The Mind–Body Connection

Performance anxiety

I am not a great golfer, by any means, but one day I had a dramatic experience on the course. On the first few holes, I parred one and bogeyed two. My friends were astonished!

Then I teed off on the fourth—a beautiful drive, straight down the middle of the fairway. As I watched the ball, I suddenly thought, "I can't wait to tell my physical therapist I'm playing pain-free! Barely a twinge!"

Then I took my next shot. I rolled it, and rolled it again. I went from a five on the fourth hole to a ten on the fifth. By the end of the eighth hole, I had tried everything to recover my form.

⊛   It was clear the problem was psychological. As soon as I thought, "I'm not having any problems with my muscles," boom! I messed up my game. The effect was immediate.

When the players are anxious about something or feel pressured, there's a systematic demise of their game, and there's no retrieving it. They begin to make mistakes, which increases their anxiety. Studies of professional athletes have shown that anxiety-producing stress can affect the ability to process visual cues. The player may miss an opportunity to pass, for example, by not seeing where another player is headed.

This is one reason it's so important for coaches and parents not to overreact to a player's mistakes. It is best to help the child brush them off. They're going to make mistakes, and we have to learn to accept them.

☺   Sometimes, the players with the most performance anxi-
     ety are those whose parents are over involved in the
     child's sport.

• *Shooter's anxiety*
     Lynn, Shari, and Christine were wonderful players who
had trouble shooting a goal. They'd miss the kick, or the ball
would go wide instead of going into the box. In each case
the problem was clearly caused by anxiety. These girls played
so well in other areas of the game.
     When players' skills fail them, it's because they're not
"in the moment." They're thinking about what's ahead—
about getting the ball in the box—instead of connecting with
the ball.
     I handled the situation with each girl in an identical
way, but separately. I had them all come early to one practice for a shooting drill, and I took each aside individually
to give her the following simple instruction: "When you go
to kick that ball, I want you to say three things to yourself,
'Relax. Concentrate. Control.' Just say those three words
throughout the drill and see what happens. And I want you
to watch the ball until your foot strikes it. Don't look at the
goalie, don't look at the box—you've already seen the box,
you know where you are in relationship to it. Simply watch
the ball until your foot kicks it away. Relax, concentrate, and
control." (This formula comes from an old self-hypnosis tape
my Dad once gave me, to help my tennis game.) After this
little speech, each player took her turn drilling, kicking balls
into the goal, while I gave the speech to the next one.
     With each girl, the drill worked like magic. One after
the other, good strong kicks into the box. Lynn kicked the
ball like I've never seen her kick before, into the top corner
of the goalie box! "WOW!" she said, beaming.

The next part of the exercise was to talk about the drill at our team meeting. The three players had a chance to tell their teammates the three words to remember in taking a kick: "Relax, concentrate, control."

Before the following game, I did a shooting drill with two of these players. I was in the box playing goalie. I told them, "I know you can do it. Just concentrate on getting the ball into the box." They made shot after shot. I said, "My god, where's this coming from?" Shari said, "I don't know!" Her success created a kind of spiral of confidence, and—sure enough—she scored our first goal.

• *Goalie anxiety*

Playing goalie is a tough job. It's scary to have someone flying at you, positioned to kick you in the face as you pick up the ball. Many goalies have trouble with the idea of sliding onto the ball for precisely that reason.

For most players, goal keeping requires desensitization drills, which can't be accomplished in general practice. In fact, goalie training is so important and so unlike other aspects of soccer training it requires at least a few special practices. The routine is simple: begin by throwing easy balls at first, and have the player master that before making the drill more difficult. Over a period of several days, the balls start to come faster and harder and from closer in, as the player masters each new level of challenge. Eventually, the goalie may have more than one attacker running directly at her, ready to boot the ball.

Desensitization requires gradual, incremental steps, so that the anxiety level is increased just enough to provide a challenge but never enough to make the player back down.

A very different aspect of goalie anxiety relates not to the physical challenge of blocking a ball but to the mental challenge of having a highly visible job to perform, single-handedly. One of our goalies, Ellen, was very susceptible to performance anxiety. She usually did well, but if she missed blocking a ball, she seemed to give up. Her body language— walking, not running, with her hands thrown up—said, "I know you're going to score, so I'm not even going to try." This is a player who was generally wonderful to coach, had a terrific attitude, and made an effort to follow directions.

Another goalie, Debby, was incredibly resilient psychologically. She took each play as a new event, a new challenge—each point as the first point. She had that first-time confidence every time. When Debby saw someone approaching the goal, it was her chance to show how good she was. Ellen, on the other hand, was afraid it would show how bad she was. When Debby succeeded in blocking a point, it was a huge satisfaction for her. If she missed a ball, that was simply a goal they managed to score. When Ellen succeeded in blocking, she felt she was merely doing her job, but every missed ball was a mistake for which she felt incredibly responsible.

Once, immediately following a game, I tried to talk to Ellen about goal keeping. She was so self-conscious about her performance she couldn't hear what I had to say. "Yeah, I know," she interrupted, "I messed that up." And she walked away. I had, in fact, wanted to praise her, but she couldn't hear it just then. This was a case in which I realized too late in the season that the player was just not suited to the position, and it was destroying her confidence.

• Fear problems

A fellow coach consulted me about his ten-year-old son, Nick, who became so afraid when another player ran at him, he backed up. This reaction is common among kids in the beginning. Some become gradually desensitized. Others become more sensitized, and their fears grow deeper.

This coach tried desensitization drills, where he'd run toward Nick—but the coach was simply too large. His size intimidated his son, and rather than desensitizing him it actually sensitized him further. As in any desensitization process, it's essential to go in small steps: dribble toward the player slowly and have him steal the ball. Make it gradually harder, over several weeks, by running faster. The rate of progress will vary with the individual, and it cannot be rushed.

⊛   In desensitizing, you need to raise the fear level very gradually so that the player can overcome it *every time*.

The challenge has to be increased over time in order for the player to improve. Some level of anxiety is necessary to bring out a player's optimum performance.

When a player has succeeded in approaching the ball rather than backing away, the coach should point that out, and ask whether he still feels the same anxiety. Help the player become conscious of his physical reactions.

Injury cycles

Coaches and parents have to address the issue of injuries when kids are young. One of the character-building lessons of athletics is learning to react to an injury rationally rather than with panic. A coach can best help the player do this by acknowledging, rather than denying, both the physical injury and the emotional distress that may accompany it.

It's sometimes difficult to know when a player is feigning injury and looking for a little TLC, and when she is honestly injured. Often, the player doesn't know for sure. With younger children, it's usually that they're scared. An important part of the coach's job is to help the player learn to listen to her body—to do a "body scan" and decide for herself whether she is really hurt.

We played one game against a team whose coach is notorious throughout the league for his overbearing style. He denigrates his players from the sidelines and badgers the referees. I've never seen as many injuries in one game as his team suffered that day. Every time we had the ball, the ref invariably stopped the game because one of their players was hurt and sitting on the field crying. As ridiculous as it sounds, I wondered if they had perhaps been coached to behave that way.

It seems likely the players were using minor injuries as an opportunity to get out of the game and perhaps get a little positive attention from the coach, who seemed genuinely concerned when they were hurt. While playing, they risked criticism. When they were injured, they were nurtured. The reason the injuries happened only when our team had the ball is obvious: if the girls gave in to an injury when their team had the ball, they were not likely to get the same kind of nurturing attention from their coach.

• *Evaluating and responding*
    The ultimate goal for a coach is to help the children realize their God-given strengths: physical, mental, and emotional. In order to accomplish this, we must provide an environment that reinforces powerful, joyful, enthusiastic play. Everyone has physical weaknesses, but the degree to which they interfere with our play often depends upon how much attention we focus on them.

This is where coaching decisions become especially tricky. Few of us are doctors, and we lack the medical expertise to assess injuries. Most of us prefer to err on the side of caution, which is appropriate. Fortunately, most of the injuries we see are minor and the pain is relatively mild.

Some children seem to get injured in just about every practice and game and their pain appears more severe and longer lasting than that of their peers. These players need assistance in shifting the focus of their attention from their vulnerabilities to their strengths. If they are not already stuck in the "I'm hurt, take care of me" cycle, they are at high risk for creating that pattern for themselves.

The reality is, no child could get stuck in this pattern of behavior without parents, coaches, or other adults reinforcing it. For this reason, the pattern is easy to mend, but it requires a commitment to consistency.

I worked with an incredibly athletic child who was an absolute joy to watch on the field. Lucia was fast and extraordinarily aggressive for a ten-year-old girl. She was passionate about the game and had a remarkable intuitive sense for strategic play. This player exhibited all the natural talents and love of sport a coach treasures. Unfortunately, much of her energy went into feeling victimized, by opponents during games and her own teammates during scrimmages. She established a pattern: "She hurt me; you help me."

In every practice, Lucia literally screamed in pain after falling to the ground, being kicked, or being pushed. Then, she would begin to cry. The most interesting part of her routine was the language she used. When asked if she was okay, she'd say, "She kicked (or tripped or pushed) me!" Her focus was not on what happened, but rather on the person who *did it to her*, as if she believed her teammate or opponent deliberately caused her injury.

Who knows why this pattern developed for this child? I've come to realize that, as a coach, it really doesn't matter why the problem arises. The important thing is for me to be as accepting and non-judgmental as I possibly can, while consciously avoiding reinforcing the child's feelings of victimization.

The solution turned out to be surprisingly easy. In the beginning, when Lucia would collapse in pain and tears during our scrimmages, the entire team would form a ring of empathy around her. "Oh Lucia, are you okay?" and "I'm sorry, Lucia" would echo from her teammates. It was touching to witness such compassion, and I often wondered what the children must have thought of my apparent indifference and lack of concern for their teammate's agony. I usually responded by telling the kids to get back to playing, while I slowly made my way over to Lucia to ask, not "What happened?" but simply, "Can you walk?" My question was very specific, because I was trying to bring Lucia's awareness back to her physical self. We both needed to know, first, whether there was a physical problem that required more attention than I was capable of providing. When it was clear that Lucia could walk, I simply said, "Why don't you walk off the field until you feel you can play." I returned immediately to the scrimmage, knowing that Lucia would eventually return in all her glory—passionate, aggressive, and beaming with power.

Soon after, our games became problem-free. Lucia began to handle her injuries without leaving the field. And eventually, she could play through every scrimmage without a major upset.

I try to be specific and consistent in the language I use when attempting to raise a child's consciousness. Creating a pattern of language that is simple and direct is necessary in order to break through the more complicated pattern of behavior that interferes with a player's game. It doesn't take long for the child to realize that the old pattern of behavior is not going to get the attention she sought, so she gives up the pattern and begins to rejoice in showing off her strengths.

- *Incapacitating fear*
    Debby's parents had gone out of town the day before one of our soccer practices and would be gone for the weekend, missing our game. Debby arrived at practice, running and skipping onto the field, saying, "My parents are away! They're not going to be at the game tomorrow." I said, "Oh, that's too bad," but it didn't occur to me that it might be a problem for her. Some of the other parents traveled and of-

ten missed games.

During a drill that afternoon, Debby took a picture out of her jeans pocket and said, "This is my big sister." I said, "Wow, she's really pretty, isn't she?" She said, "Yeah. She's not here now." I knew that her sister was away at college, and I said, "I bet you miss her." Debby nodded. Then we went on to the next drill.

At the game the next day, Debby was working hard but having trouble breathing. I thought she was tired and asked if she needed a sub. She shook her head no and stayed in the game. I realize in retrospect she probably should have come out, and that I needed to make that decision for her. Instead, I left it up to her to make the call.

⚽ I leave the physical aspects up to the individual players, unless it's clear they're not able to make the right decision. I want them to learn to judge their own situation and to know that I'll respect their judgment and follow their cues.

Later in the game, Debby was clearly fighting for breath and began crying, so I pulled her out. She became hysterical, sobbing uncontrollably. "I can't breathe!" she said. I tried to calm her and stay calm myself. Meanwhile, the game was continuing behind us. Several parents came up to offer help.

"This happened to me before!" she said. "I can't breathe!" It was at that point it hit me: her parents weren't there. "You *are* breathing," I said. "I know it feels like you can't breathe, but you are breathing, or you wouldn't be able to talk to me right now. Let's try to slow it down. Try to close your mouth." I was trying to get her back into the controlled nostril breathing she had learned in practice, but she was too hysterical. I continued to reassure her as she sat cuddled next to me. I knew that the crying could also help to slow her breathing.

☺   The biggest part of a coach's job may be taking care of
     emotional issues as they arise, especially in coaching
     younger children.

Debby continued to cry, but she began to say "I couldn't
breathe" instead of "I can't breathe." So I said, "You were
out on the field and you couldn't breathe?" "Yeah, I couldn't
breathe!" Then she began to cry harder. I said, "I see. Right
now you can breathe but you're still remembering how
scared you were on the field. Is that what you're saying?" "I
was scared, I was so scared. I'm scared!" she sobbed. "Yeah,
that's a scary feeling. I've had that many times myself, when
you get the feeling that you can't breathe. And the more
frightened you get about it the more you can't breathe,
right?" "Yes," she said, crying even harder. "Well, the good
thing is, that part of it is over. It's good that we know right
now you're crying because you're scared that you *couldn't*
breathe, and we know that part of it is over. You can breathe
now. But it's still scary, right?" "Yeah."

Within a few minutes, she was calm again. The crisis
was resolved.

The other parents tried to get Debby to stay with them
while the game continued, but I felt it was better for her to
stay with me. There's no substitute for a child's parents, but
you take the next best thing. At that time, as her coach, I was
probably the next best thing. So Debby stayed with me for
the rest of the first half, going up and down the sidelines. In
the second half, she went back in as goalie.

• *The psychological factor in recurrent injuries*

Liz sometimes collapsed during games with minor injuries, leaving the field in tears—although there was never
an evident sign of physical injury. Other times, she took hard
hits and kept playing. It occurred to me that when her dad
wasn't present at a game Liz played without injury. I won-

dered whether she was afraid of making a mistake and being yelled at when her dad was there and subconsciously looked for a chance to get out of the game.

⚽ Injuries can serve an avoidance function for a fearful player.

On my niece's soccer team, there was one player who would be carried off the field, screaming and crying, whenever she fell during a game—and that was the end of the game for her. The coach was a doctor, and he would ice the knee each time (it was consistently her knee). Isabel always cried as if in excruciating pain and claimed to be unable to return to play—although the injury was never severe enough to keep her out of the next game.

One day, as Isabel lay crying on the sidelines, I walked over to her, knelt down, and said, "So it's that knee again, huh? What happened to it?" "I don't know." "Is it the same one you hurt last week?" "I don't know!" "I noticed that you hurt your knees a couple of times." Isabel said, "Yeah, and everybody in my family has knee problems, and they've all had surgery. My dad had surgery, my sister's had surgery, my brother has a knee problem, and now I have knee problems."

Isabel's parents were obviously treating the recurring incidents as a knee problem, but it appeared to be the fear of having a knee problem. Real or imagined, it was a debilitating problem for this young athlete. If allowed to continue, this fear could eventually lead to real injury.

⚽ Isabel's fear of injury seemed independent of any actual physical problem. My advice to her parents would be to stand her up, brush off the knees, assure her there's nothing wrong, and put her back in the game before her fear of injury is established as a pattern.

I watched a whole season of games in which a friend's son participated. The team was made up of thirteen- and fourteen-year-old boys. The star player, Mark, happened to be the coach's son. Mark was a gifted athlete, with physical strength, speed, and skill beyond most kids his age. It was evident this young man had extraordinary natural ability, as well as superior coaching from his dad.

I noticed something unusual about Mark's game, however. He would play extraordinarily well until the last ten or fifteen minutes of each game. At that point, he would suffer an incapacitating injury, so serious he would be carried off the field by his dad. His mother, on the sidelines, would go to him and pat his forehead while he lay curled in the fetal position, crying.

I was astonished at the level of attention paid to all these injuries and at the obliviousness to their predictability. When I asked another parent what was going on, I was told, "Mark really plays hard out there," followed by a detailed account of the incident in that particular game.

Finally, in the last game of the season, my friend admitted, "It's hard to tell what's going on. He's a little dramatic." Indeed he was, and his dramatic sense included an uncanny awareness of how much time was left in the game (though he didn't wear a watch). Mark was able to assure himself of ample playing time every week, and still fit in these regular demonstrations for TLC.

Considering the sheer delight parents feel in their children's abilities and strengths, from the time the toddler takes his first step, it is curious to see parents unwittingly encourage a return to helplessness and dependency. A psychologist might want to analyze the family dynamic at work, but as a coach I simply observe that Mark's extraordinary soccer skills would be better accompanied by stronger life skills. The coach could begin by requesting he walk off the field instead of carrying him, and his mother could be less responsive to his pleas for negative reinforcement.

• *The psychological impact of physical injuries*
    I strongly advise parents to give kids the opportunity for sports. I will go so far as to say, push them strongly into some athletic endeavor. But make sure you give them something else along the way. Make sure they're defined in other ways than just by their sport.

⊛   The sport is not who your child is. Children have other interests: art, science, music, whatever. It's important not to put so much emphasis on their athletic abilities that it overshadows everything else.

Later in life, when an athlete has to deal with an injury that stops her game, a sense of identity can become a major problem: who am I, now that this injury has put a stop to my sport? A major injury that prevents the competitive athlete from playing for months—or, in the worst case, for life—could very likely be the most traumatic and potentially depressing experience of her life. Nevertheless, the athlete needs to take the time to take care of a physical problem so it doesn't become a bigger problem. The team will survive without her.

• *Coaches in denial*
    Whatever the cost to the team, a player must take time out from her sport for an injury to heal.
    In the 1996 Olympic gymnastics competition, it sickened me to see a young athlete who had clearly injured her ankle go back to vault again! The USA won the gold medal—but was it worth it? What additional damage did the young woman do to the injury?
    The daughter of my friend Rita was playing in a competitive league that had an important tournament coming up.

In an earlier game, one of the players, Karina, had suffered a major bone fracture. The coaches called Karina's mother to ask that she have her daughter attend the tournament as a spectator. Karina was still on strict bedrest, unable to go to school or even ride in a car, under doctor's orders. Nevertheless, she showed up at the tournament!

Rita, who has medical training, confronted Karina's mother. "What are you doing? Why did you bring your daughter here?" The mother responded, "The coaches wanted her to come, and she wanted to see the game." "But didn't the doctor put her on strict bedrest?" "Yes, he did, but the coaches kept calling and I just felt I had to do it—they really wanted her here." "Do you realize," Rita asked in amazement, "that your daughter could end up back in the hospital?" "I know," was the answer. My friend walked away in disgust.

I am in favor of players attending their team's games even when they are unable to play—so long as it isn't going to do them any harm. This practice is healthy, both for the team and for the player. But in Karina's case, when a coach usurps the physician's authority and the parent complies with the coach's wishes, there is something seriously wrong with both the parent and the coach.

Karina undoubtedly sat on the sidelines that day in agonizing pain, unaware of additional damage caused by the effort.

Wouldn't the team's morale have been boosted more by seeing the coach's concern for the player's health? No one can dispute the warmth and comfort we feel when someone puts our welfare first. Wouldn't this be a wonderful message to give the entire team?

The team experience is important, but only to the extent that it enhances the individual's life experience and contributes to her self-love and self-respect—to the extent that the sport helps her realize her gifts as a person.

⊕   On the one hand, we just brush off the knees of our
players and send them back into the game (when they
need to understand that what they are suffering is not
physical pain). On the other hand, we have to stop them
from playing when doing so would exacerbate an injury.

When a team sport becomes a damaging experience for
a team member, the fault lies with the coach and parents. As
coaches, we have to keep things in perspective. Karina's
coaches could have said, "We'll videotape the game for you,
and we'd like you to think about us during that time. We'll
bring over the videotape, set it up, and the team will watch
it with you." In the case of serious injury, the coach's responsibility is to see what the team can do for the player, not the
other way around. As a parent, the welfare of the child must
always be your number one concern.

• *Adapting to physical limitations*
Following my assault, physical injuries made it impossible for me to do the things I once enjoyed—hiking, running,
cycling, and playing tennis. I went from a high level of fit-
ness and activity to complete inactivity.
One of my favorite activities had been a daily hike in
Great Falls National Park on the Potomac River. After the attack, I would drive to the river and sit by the rocks, about
an eighth of a mile from the parking lot. There were days,
however, when I couldn't even do that. On those days, I
would get out of the car and sit in a spot just three minutes
away from the car. It wasn't much, but it was something. I
had no choice but to make adjustments according to my
physical limitations.
For a young athlete, some willingness to adapt and
make changes may be necessary at times. The world has a
lot to offer outside the realm of sports. The same positive

outlook and determination that were crucial in athletics can help the injured athlete pursue new goals and opportunities.

Developing the mind-body connection
• *"Kathy, the plane will fly itself"*

I became interested in flying at sixteen, when I was recovering from surgery and unable to participate in sports. My dad and I went out in his plane twice a week. He knew how important it was to me, and the fact that he was able to take the time to go with me was a big deal.

I'd get the plane up in the air and try to follow a certain heading, but it's tricky because a propeller plane wants to climb. You have to learn to maneuver so you don't overshoot the turn, while keeping the plane from climbing. I remember watching my dad as he piloted, amazed at how graceful he was. When I was flying I was very animated, putting everything I had into it. By the time I landed, I was exhausted. But my dad never flexed a muscle. I recall one time putting my hand on his forearm and asking, "How come your muscles aren't working?" He said, "Kathleen, the plane will fly itself. Don't try to fly it. All you have to do as a pilot is guide. The plane will do all the work."

That theory applies to almost anything in life. If you're mindful of what you're doing at each moment, things will proceed with almost no effort. Getting the players to do what they need to on the soccer field without exerting unnecessary effort is a huge task. But it can be done, and, with practice, the skills will begin to feel natural to them.

• *Take care of the feelings first*

At one of our practices, Susan, Christine, and Debby ended up in tears. These three girls never cried unless there was real injury. Each of them had wiped out on a number of occasions and just got up and kept going.

On that particular day, Susan was hit in the stomach by

the ball. That can be scary even for an adult. Susan was crying inconsolably, but I felt it was more fear than physical pain. All the girls ran to her, and, as always, Dave told them sternly to move away to give the injured player space.After Dave had soothed Susan's fears and she was calm again, he said, "Okay, let's go."

That is a really good approach: take care of the feelings first, then put the player back into action.

The same thing happened with Christine: she was hit in the leg by the ball. She was wearing shorts, and since it was a very cold day, the hit stung. She started to cry. With Christine too, it appeared to be shock more than physical pain that made her cry. Once her fears calmed, she was fine and ready to return to play.

At that age, kids often continue to cry even when the physical pain is over, because they were so scared when the incident happened. I made it a point to acknowledge the fear by saying, "It's pretty scary seeing that great big ball coming at you, isn't it?"

It's important to nurture the players, but we also want to help them gain control of their reactions—not by telling them, "Be brave" or "It's not so bad, you're okay," but by helping them understand when it's their fear or actual injury that has caused the reaction. This mind-body connection should be a major focus of coaches and parents.

⊕ The playing field is a good place to focus on maintaining the mind-body connection. In sports, we're constantly having to address the issue of emotional versus physical responses.

• *Reading the body language*
Debby caught on to things really quickly. She was not a player who needed to spend ten practices on one skill. So it took me by surprise when, in trying to teach a side kick I

figured she'd get right away, she was all over the place. I kept saying, "Pay attention," but she couldn't seem to concentrate long enough to receive the instruction she needed to get it right.

After the first few times I said, "Debby, pay attention! You're not even trying!" She threw her arms up and yelled, "Wait!" I realized then there was something else on her mind and she was doing her best that day. She was working really hard but she couldn't store the sequence long enough to mimic it. So each time she tried, I just said, "Way to go" or "Okay, that's better, much better."

Later in the game, she came to me complaining of a headache. That was unlike Debby. I asked if she needed to sit out, but she said no. So I said, "Is your head hurting because you had a bad day at school?" And she said, "No, my head hurts, it really hurts. I think I'm getting sick," and she looked as if she would cry. I said, "If you need to sit out, sit out, but I need to continue these drills." So I continued, and she decided to stay in the drills.

When Debby's mom dropped her off at the next practice I learned there had indeed been a problem at school, serious enough that her mother had kept her home until she could take it up with the teacher and principal. This was a situation in which the child's body language proved a reliable guide to her state of mind.

• *Visualization*

I took the time at one rainy day team meeting to ask the players about their psychological game. At this age, when they develop a passion for an activity they may also imagine themselves performing at an optimum level—as a star. This can be a powerful tool for their development, since half the game is psychological.

I asked how many of them sometimes imagined themselves playing soccer, how many imagined themselves dribbling past the opposing team, making great passes, winning the ball, scoring a goal? The hands shot up everywhere. Several talked about how, on the night before a game, they would imagine themselves playing really well, scoring goals, and some even dreamed about it.

Interestingly, the only one who said she never visualized a great performance was one of our more skillful players. Despite her skill, this player lacked the natural competitiveness some of the others exhibited.

I then talked about making this sort of visualization part of their practice: "Try to imagine, or visualize, yourself dribbling down the field, through several opponents, with perfect control of your game." If players use this technique enough, they will actually be able to do what they visualize.

CHAPTER FIVE
Managing Practices and Games

There seems to be no end to the possibilities in coaching kids, no end to how much you can learn from one practice to the next that will change your approach. The following techniques worked well for us—most of the time.

Maintaining order

Having observed team practices in baseball, basketball, and soccer involving third-, fourth-, and fifth-grade girls and boys, I think it's accurate to say that kids can be very difficult to manage! Every coach's biggest problem is getting them to pay attention. At first I tried the usual: "LISTEN!!" If I succeeded in silencing them this way, it only lasted about thirty seconds before someone would start goofing around. Then I decided to talk over them—which, of course, was a complete waste of energy. How could I talk over twelve energetic kids?

Finally I gave up trying to get their attention and just said, "Okay, tell me when you're ready. When you're ready I'll speak, but I won't keep trying to talk over you. You come to me when the whole team is ready."

Pretty soon Lisa came to where I stood and said, "We're ready now." "Who is ready?" I asked. "The team is ready," she said. "How many of you are there?" I asked. "Twelve." "How many are here now?" "One," she said. "So then our team isn't ready, is it?"

This method had great success. Silence from me gave them nothing to fight against, nothing to overpower. It eliminated the conflict between coach and players by putting the responsibility in the hands of the players. The disruptive kids were whipped into shape by those who were ready to listen.

We formalized this arrangement by assigning practice captains.

• *Practice captains*

Trying to manage twelve ten-year-old girls is a real task. Invariably, you get one quieted down and another starts up. You get one drill team ready to go, but the other one's completely clueless because they've been clowning around. Dave and I came up with a plan to handle the situation.

We told the girls we would have a fifteen-minute scrimmage at the end of every practice, provided we were able to get through the drills we had prepared for that day. If, because of their lack of participation, we were not able to complete the drills in the time allotted, the extra time needed would come out of their scrimmage. Every minute they wasted would cost them a minute of their scrimmage. This system worked really well.

⚽   If the team worked hard they had their full scrimmage time, but if they clowned around they lost that amount of time out of their scrimmage (the activity they loved the most).

I added a twist to the plan. Instead of trying to get the players into order myself, I assigned two practice captains (one on each drill team) on a rotating basis. Their job was to keep their drill team listening during practice.

The first day I used this technique, I deliberately chose one of my worst listeners to serve as one captain and the player I thought listened the most consistently as the second. It worked amazingly well. As soon as I felt the players weren't listening, I'd stop talking. The practice captains would immediately say, "C'mon guys, we gotta be quiet. Pay attention!" It was great!

The players paid more attention to each other than to me, so this served to keep the power with the players themselves. Jessica, the consistently good listener, seemed to enjoy the job. A couple of times she was actually one of the ones clowning around, and when I became silent, she giggled and said "Okay, okay. We have to pay attention now."

I had wondered how they would react to having practice captions. I was pleasantly surprised when, at the end of the first practice, several of them asked, "Can I be the practice captain next time?" I assured them the position would rotate—at each practice there would be two practice captains, and there were enough practices left that they would all get a turn. It's wonderful to see how kids take responsibility when it's given to them.

• *Silent drills*

It's always hard to keep kids focused when they're standing in line, waiting a turn to perform a drill. In general, it's best to avoid drills that require waiting a turn, though sometimes it's unavoidable.

One day, as a method of teaching the players to concentrate, I told them to practice the shooting drill without speaking (except, of course, for the person receiving, who had to call out). "If I catch you talking, I'm going to—" and I stopped, because I didn't have any idea what I was going to do. So I said, "Let me ask you guys, what do you think I should do?"

Right away, several suggested, "Laps. You should make them run laps!" Lisa said, "I don't think that's a good idea, because when we all have to run a lap because someone was talking, somebody always says 'Gee, thanks a lot!' to the one who did it. And if I were the one, it wouldn't feel very good." "And," I said, "I want to keep lap-running for conditioning, not for punishment."

Someone suggested, "The person who's talking loses time off their scrimmage each time you catch them." "But it's unfair to the rest of the scrimmage team," said another, "if one person is sitting out." "It's fair," I answered. "You're part of that scrimmage team. You make sure your teammate doesn't talk!"

Lynn had an idea: "This is sort of crazy but it would work. If someone talks, have the person run over to the side of the field and pick fifty clover flowers! . . . No, wait, that's too many. Twenty-five." "No. That's silly," another said. "Have them lose five minutes of scrimmage for each time they're caught." "But that's a lot of time," I reminded them, "because we only have fifteen or twenty minutes of scrimmage. Suppose we say two minutes." "Let's combine them," one player offered. "Kathy will decide each time whether the person has to pick flowers or lose scrimmage time."

On the first day we tried this, three picked flowers and three lost scrimmage time; one did both. It was pretty light-hearted, but it was enough of a punishment to keep them in line and focused (for the most part) on what they were doing.

• *The Sub Box*

Perhaps every coach has had to deal with one or more players who simply cannot contain their impatience to go into the game and who follow the coach up and down the sidelines begging, "When can I go in? Can I go in? Let me go in, *pleeeease!*" Who would want to stifle this sort of enthusiasm?

I chose to contain it instead (and preserve my sanity) by using a sub box. This was simply a space on the sidelines, about five feet by eight feet, marked out in a rough rectangle by four orange cones. Players were to remain inside the rectangle when they were not in the game, if they wanted to be subbed back in.

This approach allowed me to focus on the game, and

gave me quick access to eager, ready subs when needed. My brother-in-law has borrowed this technique and now won't do without it. "When it's time to sub," he said, "I'm able to get my thoughts together and go over to tell the players when they will go in. The ones coming off the field go right into the sub box, and that's the end of that!"

• *Drill stations*

The idea of drill stations occurred to Dave and me when confronting the lack of time to practice all the necessary skills. The group is too large and the time too limited (one and a half hours) to allow enough ball handling for each player. We had already split the group into two teams to work on different skills, but dealing with five or more players each was still too many.

Also, it was clear to us that most of the team members were not practicing on their own—because they couldn't motivate themselves to practice alone, couldn't see the value in it, or didn't know where to begin.

The drill stations provided a way to maximize each player's ball handling, allowing for practice on important ball skills on a regular basis. It also resolved the problem of players' inability to practice on their own.

We set up five stations, with three kids at each. Each station practiced a different skill: changes of direction, fakes, passing and dribbling, shooting, one-touch shots on goal. This system worked remarkably well. The stations that focused on dribbling skills and quick changes of direction required individual work, which gave the girls constant touch on the ball for the entire time they were at that station. The other stations worked on passing, receiving, and shooting skills. There too they were active the whole time and had a lot of contact with the ball. The girls changed stations about every seven minutes, which seemed to keep them motivated. The variety energized them. They were forced to work really hard on a particular drill because the time was so limited. They didn't have a chance to get bored and start goofing around, because just when their attention was maxed out, they switched to a new station. The new station then required fresh concentration and provided a new challenge.

This type of practice is not without its share of problems. We realized quickly that certain drills needed more supervision to be useful. Anything new needs to be done with close supervision at first, so the kids know exactly what they are practicing and they receive correction as they go along. The drills also needed to be easily contained in a small area. We tried a two-on-one drill, running from mid-field to the goal, but it was a disaster because the space to be covered was too large. The girls had difficulty staying on task, and a great deal of time was wasted chasing balls and arguing about who did what. We changed this station immediately to a pass and one-touch shot into the goal, which kept them confined to a smaller area with a repetitive task—ideal for this type of practice.

After a couple of weeks, we asked the players for feedback on the drill stations. They all found the system valuable, they said. They had been able to practice more on their own at home because they knew what to do. They appreciated getting more touches on the ball. They also found that going over the same skills at every practice was helping them improve. A couple of the girls pointed out the importance of devoting some practice time to drills that require a coach's presence and supervision.

It's always good to ask the players for feedback, but only if the coach has a genuine interest in hearing their opinions. Coaches need to be able to hear what the players would like changed and then make changes where appropriate. In most cases, I have found that the players give honest assessments, citing both the positives and negatives as they see them. Obviously there will be times when coaches will pull rank, as coaches have knowledge the players can't appreciate. Without the insight of the players, however, a team cannot develop as well.

• *Incentives*

Our goal as coaches is to encourage a healthy transition for the players, from practicing to please others (coaches, parents, teachers, grandparents) to practicing for themselves. We strive to promote this independence, even while we understand how difficult this transition can be for a ten-year old.

Dave and I provided an incentive, one that rewarded the entire drill team for practicing well without constant supervision. The drill team that practiced the hardest and most productively—meaning, they didn't get off task, they resolved disputes among themselves quickly, and they never stopped practicing until they switched stations—got to serve as captains for our next game. (We had two game captains plus a warm-up captain at every game.)

During our team time at the end of practice, I announced which group I thought practiced most productively, giving specific examples of what they did well (didn't waste time switching stations, made decisions quickly and cooperatively, etc.). Giving specific examples lets everyone know that you honestly observed and evaluated them, while it makes the team more aware of what you are striving for. Without such specific accounts, the praise would not be as powerful, and in fact might shift attention away from their accomplishments to focus on the reward instead. The players love to be recognized for their efforts, and they deserve to get specific, positive feedback on the areas they manage well during practice.

Special tasks
• *Toe kickers*

Three of our players continued to use their toes to kick

the ball despite constant correction from Dave and me. A toe kicker's ball will rarely get to the intended receiver. In fact, it will go almost anywhere *except* to the receiver—and it is the receiver who has to fetch the ball that was booted fifteen to twenty feet wide. It's frustrating for the players as well as for the coaches.

We finally realized that these toe kickers had established a pattern and were not going to change, so we decided to team the three together during drill stations. Not only was this fair to the other players, it also gave the offending players the valuable experience of looking in the mirror at their own mistakes. In addition, we wanted their teammates to know that we empathized with their frustrations. And we felt it was time to remove ourselves from an active coaching role on this problem.

When I assigned the drill teams, I explained that Leslie, Chris, and Nora would work together at each practice, because they had been unable to break the habit of using their toes to kick the ball, and we could no longer allow this bad habit to disrupt the team's valuable practice time. When these players changed the habit and began to kick properly, they would be worked back into the other groups.

I had considered talking to these girls separately to let them know why they would be grouped together, keeping the discussion out of the team process. I am not in favor of publicly humiliating anyone, especially children, and I realized that presenting the plan to the group as a whole might result in the three feeling embarrassed. I decided it was worth risking their discomfort if it might push them to focus on a change that would benefit the team.

One of the toe kickers approached Dave during this practice and said, "You know, I'm not *trying* to use my toe," to which he responded, "Well, maybe now you'll make yourself stop."

By the end of the second practice, the three had made

great progress and began to call my attention to their instep kicking: "Look! Is this right?" Once they had broken the habit, I made it a point to let the team know they would be joining the team in switching drill partners.

I had spent an entire season pulling my hair out, trying to get these kids to use their insteps, and was completely ineffective. All I had to do was put the onus on them and walk away. Making the team aware of when an individual's participation is not satisfactory can be a powerful incentive to bring about change.

• *Picking partners*

I never tell the kids to pair up for drills. I always assign partners. At this age, girls are starting to form cliques and I know what would happen if they chose their own partners. They'd get together with their friends, and some girls would feel left out. It's important to keep building the team experience and have each player work with every other player.

On the other hand, Dave often says simply, "Pair up." That can also be a useful exercise, and it allows me to observe periodically what's happening with the team—which girls are still not completely part of the group.

Motivating players
• *External incentives*

All coaches have dealt with players who need some type of external motivation to get past the sort of unfocused participation that distracts the rest of the team. These kids range from being overtly disruptive to subtly mindless, preventing them from developing with their team. While the former is impossible to ignore, the latter can be very difficult to detect.

As young kids just beginning to play tennis, my siblings and I regularly struggled with an inertia problem. Since we hadn't yet developed the level of play that inspires an athlete to practice, my dad would bribe us by letting us have a soda after playing an hour of tennis. For most children today, this particular incentive would not make an impression, because they get soda all the time, but for us it was a real treat. Many times, when my turn for tennis rolled around, I wouldn't feel like playing. My dad would say, "Well, okay then, there's no soda for you tonight." All he had to do was remind me of what I was giving up, and I was off and running for my tennis racket. That small reward was enough to keep us developing our tennis game until we were at the level of play where we derived such satisfaction from it we wanted to play all the time and didn't need any other incentive. I have to wonder if I would ever have gotten past the hacking stage without that reward.

I heard recently of a tennis coach who successfully used pushups to make his players stop returning serves into the net. Andrew, who according to the coach was easily returning balls served at 100 miles per hour, consistently returned every serve because he wasn't about to do pushups! This coach was able to use the threat of doing pushups to get his players to concentrate more, thereby raising their performance. He was helping his players discover the glory of mindfulness (keeping their heads in the game).

My approach is more like my father's. He would simply provide an image, such as, "Focus on the ball hitting the strings of your racket." I prefer this approach because it directly enhances the player's focus, whereas the threat of lap running or pushups shifts the player's attention away from the task at hand. In soccer, I will tell a player, "Concentrate on your foot striking the ball." This is a simple, direct technique for developing mindfulness.

At nine- or ten-years old, kids begin performing difficult skills just for the challenge. But some may need an incentive to get them interested in the activity in the first place—as my Dad did, giving us a soda for playing an hour of tennis.

I know of two cases in which parents used very similar methods to motivate their kids to score. A friend's daughter played on a competitive soccer team for about five years with a coach who focused on developing a few key players, while letting others sit on the bench. The benched players were occasionally allowed a few minutes of playing time at the end of a half or the end of the game. As Rose's mom tells it, "The kid just gets in the game and starts to warm up when he's pulling her out!" Moreover, she says, "this coach tells them what to do all the time, so they don't even think for themselves. They all wait for his orders."

Not surprisingly, rather than gaining confidence in herself over the years, Rose has lost the confidence she brought to the soccer field at age ten. A natural athlete, this young woman plays many different sports competitively. Her mom has watched with great concern as her daughter's confidence has eroded, to the point where Rose would not even attempt to shoot the ball. Whether in soccer, basketball, or field hockey, Rose "will bring it all the way down and then pass it off."

As we talked I wondered aloud if there was anything that could be used to shift Rose's focus from her internal belief that she is no good—some external motivation that would inspire her to shoot. Once a player is locked into a self-defeating cycle, we can't just tell them to change. In fact, as we focus attention on the fact that the child has no confidence, we may further damage her confidence.

Imagine a child who doesn't shoot because of her belief that she is no good. A new coach tells her she's great and that she needs to start shooting. The player does what the coach wants her to do and shoots—still believing she is going to blow it. With such a strong belief that she will not succeed, she can't succeed. Now the child has tried and blown it, convincing her that she can't shoot. The self-defeating cycle is established.

⊛ If there was something external Rose could use to shift her attention away from the problem, she stood a great chance of overcoming the obstacle.

The following season, in field hockey, Rose's dad came up with a brilliant idea: he would give her five dollars per goal for the entire season. Rose's mom had some reservations about "paying our kid to score" but decided to "just see if she could do it for something external." This enabled Rose to simply shoot for money. If she failed, she would not be losing more of herself, she just wouldn't be gaining five dollars. If, however, she were successful, it might be enough to break the self-defeating cycle. This external motivation worked very well, and I am pleased to hear that Rose made *some bucks* playing high school field hockey! Within only a few weeks of shooting "for the green," Rose was on the way to believing in herself again.

John, playing on a competitive soccer team, had been scoring pretty regularly. One Saturday, his dad promised him a video game he wanted if he scored three goals in one game. I caught the second half of John's game, and was surprised to see him looking down after his team's victory. When I asked what was bothering him, his mother told me of the agreement he and his father had made. Since he hadn't scored three goals, he wouldn't be getting his video game.

I didn't think much of this until a conversation the following week with one of my soccer teammates, whose son is on the same team with John. She said, "Poor John. He really got yelled at today. I felt bad for him." I was surprised to hear this because he is such a good player. My friend explained that John refused to pass the ball; he kept holding on to it, trying to score. Their coach, exasperated after several unsuccessful attempts to get John to pass the ball, finally started screaming at him, "John, for once, would you please pass the ball!" Even this failed, as John continued holding on to the ball.

Needless to say, John seriously jeopardized the team's victory, because he was so focused on scoring enough goals to get his video game. In this case, an external motivation interfered with a player's performance and the team's scoring potential.

CHAPTER SIX
Maintaining the Dignity of the Team

My first experience of coaching soccer was assisting my brother-in-law, Michael. I'll never forget a valuable lesson he taught me.

Just before one of our games, as we waited for the previous game to finish, Michael was approached by the opposing coach. Games for fourth-graders are normally played with opposing teams of seven. This coach happened to have only five of his players present. Playing seven against five obviously gave us an enormous advantage.

I hadn't heard any of the discussion between the two coaches, and when it came time to play I was shocked to see Michael send in only five players. "What are you doing?" I protested. "We need seven!" "They only have five," he told me. "Well, that's their problem, isn't it?" Michael answered, "I can't outplay them; that's not fair. We have to be fair about this, so we'll do five on five. If their players come later, we'll add." "I guess you're right," I said. But as I walked away I was thinking, "Gee, we could probably win this game if we put the seven players out there." I was caught up in the idea of winning, and Michael reminded me what was important for the kids: equal and fair games.

Now, there's a good coach!

Competitiveness

My mother has often told the story of her first experience playing miniature golf, as a high school student. When she and her friends tallied up the score she could hardly contain her glee—but contain herself she did, since she didn't want to hurt her friends' feelings by exulting in her own success. At home that evening, she told her mom, "I won! I got the highest score!" It was up to her mother to explain to her the unhappy truth—golf is the one sport in which the person with the lowest score wins.

Misunderstandings aside, perceptions have a lot to do with the experience of winning and losing. Competition can bring out the best in us: our determination to succeed and the sheer joy of accomplishment (such as my mother felt on seeing her score). It can also bring out the worst, when our ego requires external reinforcement and needs others to recognize our accomplishment. This outward-focused competitiveness takes pleasure not only in winning but also in the fact that someone else has lost.

The competitiveness of kids' sports can be scary. I've had parents tell me it's a disgrace how competitive soccer has become in our area, that parents and coaches are putting too much emphasis on winning and losing. It would certainly be nice if we could follow the old saying "It's not whether you win or lose but how you play the game."

You can't go anywhere in the Washington, D.C., suburbs on a Saturday or Sunday without seeing a few soccer uniforms—unless it's pouring rain and games have been canceled. I've caught myself many times, when I run into soccer players (standing in line at an ice cream store, for example), asking them, "How was the game? Did you win?" That's what I ask, "Did you win?" When I've been with my niece after her games, that's what people always ask her. "Did you win today?" They're just being friendly and making conversation, noticing she's a soccer player.

One day, as I was about to ask the same question, I caught myself. Why is it, I wondered, that we all ask, "Did you win today?" Why can't we ask, "How was your game today? Was it fun?" Even in such casual questions, we convey what we consider important. I have become more aware of what I'm asking. Nevertheless, when my mother has attended my niece's or nephew's game, I'll ask her, "How did they do?" and she'll say, "They did great." And then I have to ask, "Did they win? Did they lose? What was the score?"

• *Positive and negative competition*

It is unfortunate that we have come to think of competition—and competitive people—as being inherently cutthroat, disrespectful, or abusive. In fact, competition is a wonderful thing, as long as it's conducted with dignity and integrity—when it is focused inward rather than outward.

When we say that competition is a bad thing, what we are really saying is too many people handle competition in a bad way. The athlete's focus should be on outdoing herself and improving her level of play every time out, not on outdoing the other player. A competitor with dignity and integrity keeps herself in focus and, when beaten, applauds her opponent.

⊛   When we say that sports are too competitive, what we're really saying is they lack integrity and dignity.

My friend's daughter, Cynthia, had just played in a major college soccer tournament. Cynthia called her mother after the tournament and said, "You know, this is the first time I've played soccer and was able to just enjoy playing the game, in all the years I've played." My friend told me that all of Cynthia's coaches had emphasized winning as the most important part of the game. Every time she went out to play, she had to win. When her team lost a game, she felt like a failure.

Cynthia started playing soccer in elementary school, so when she finished college at twenty-two, she had played the game for more than twelve years. For at least twelve years this young woman was so pressured to win she was not able to enjoy the sport.

It's possible to compete in sports without focusing on winning. If an athlete plays the best game she can play for that day, at that time, she shouldn't feel bad about herself if the team doesn't win that game. Competition is wonderful. It helps us discover who we are. It pushes us to our limits and keeps us striving for improvement. But the focus of competition has to be on developing our personal performance, not on overpowering another person.

You can tell when kids are getting the message that they have to outdo their opponent just to win, and when they're getting the message that the important thing is to play the best game they can play to the last second on the clock. When they come off the field—whether they have won or lost the game—if they focused on themselves, they look victorious. They know that this time they played better than last time, and in that way they have won.

In coaching young people, I have sometimes been guilty of focusing my attention on outdoing the other team. (This is especially a problem for coaches in competitive leagues, when a team can be dropped if it finishes last.) I have had to keep pulling myself back into focus and concentrate on our team's strengths.

Outward-focused competition is easy to recognize. In giving the standard team pep talk, a coach may pump up the negative energy instead of bringing out the positive energy, by using negative images. "You're gonna get out there, you're gonna beat those girls, run them over." These statements focus on things to do *to* the other team.

Coaches who strive to get the team to focus their competitiveness inward will give a very different sort of pep talk. "Let's do some good passing. Communicate with your team members. Be sure to support when somebody has the ball; get into position to support her in case she needs to discharge it. Back one another up. Talk to each other out there. And let's really do our best as a team."

Outward-focused competition is damaging to all involved. It's a source of animosity, humiliation, and destructiveness in our lives, whether at work, in social situations, or in our personal relationships. Inward-focused competition cultivates joy, enthusiasm, trust, and honesty.

• *Overaggressive coaches*

The coach of a team in my brother-in-law's soccer league established an incentive system to encourage his players to work harder. This coach told his team that when they won a game he would take them all for ice cream. He saw this as a way of motivating them. I see it as a way of taking away their own motivation, their joy in playing well. He was taking the fun out of the game by putting pressure on them to win. He was also setting up a situation where he could punish them when they lost by not taking them for ice cream. The message, from this coach, is that winning is the most important thing.

This sort of approach (outward-focused competition) is bound to create hostility and animosity. And that is exactly how it turned out with this particular team when it played against my brother-in-law's team. When this coach's team lost, the players became belligerent, yelling at Michael's players, who yelled back. It escalated till the coaches and parents were yelling at one another.

On the last day of that season, this same team had the field just before Michael's team played. For Michael's team, this was the decisive game for the league trophy, as all players were aware. The other team decided to stay and watch the play-off game. The coach, the players, and the parents of this team sat on the sidelines, heckling Michael's team throughout the game.

This coach clearly felt it was okay to systematically demoralize another team of ten-year olds, because he wanted to see his team win the trophy. We tend to label this sort of attitude "childish," but it isn't childish at all. Children do not destroy one another in their play. The destructive element comes from the adults, not the kids.

The soccer organization handled this situation by asking for letters from Michael and the other coach describing the episode, and then responding to each in a letter stating that their behavior was inappropriate. This approach was no doubt intended to be even-handed, but fairness would have required a reprimand to the offending coach, not to Michael who was literally minding his business.

The soccer organization showed no interest in dealing with the underlying issue of sportsmanship. There was no follow-up. There should have been a mechanism in place for bringing the coaches together, with the referees, for a hearing by an organization representative. Although the referees were alerted at the time of the heckling, they took no action. The problem was instead "resolved" bureaucratically, by putting the two teams into different leagues the following season.

• *Pressure to win*
My brother told me about his son's championship baseball game. The kids played their hearts out and did really well, but they lost.

It was sickening, he told me later, to watch what transpired afterwards. The kids were feeling okay. They believed they had played a good game and were proud they'd gotten that far, having made it all the way to the championship. But then their coaches called them together and gave them a spiel about how unfortunate it was they didn't win after they'd made it that far—one coach was actually crying! This was an *adult* coach saying to his team, "We failed because we didn't win." As my brother watched, the kids walked away upset, some of them crying. This would have been a perfect opportunity for the coach to boost the team up, to talk about what a great season it had been and how well they had played.

When our team first formed, the girls were not working together in practice; they were all over the place. They lost the first game and walked away at the end feeling pretty lousy that they'd been beaten. A few weeks into the season, after they'd begun working well together, I watched them walk away from a really good loss—a game in which they had played fantastic soccer but were beaten—and they still felt good.

I always focused on the play rather than the score. During games, the girls often asked me, "What's the score?" and I had no idea most of the time. I did not make it part of my half-time speech—ever. I never said to them, "We need two goals." When they got cocky about scores, I said, "The battle's never over until the last shot is fired. That team could come back and beat us. So just keep playing well and forget about the score. Just keep your teamwork going. It's working. You're seeing the results."

At the last game of the season, none of us (including the coach!) had any idea what our team's record was—until the conference coordinator came over to me and said, "I guess you know that if you win this game, you win the division—you'll win the trophies." When I answered, "No, actually, I don't know, I don't have a clue," he laughed in disbelief. I decided not to tell the parents or the girls at that point. The standings had not played a part in our season, and I didn't want the issue to dominate our last game. I wanted the girls to keep doing what they were doing. If it worked and we won, fantastic. If we didn't win, that would be fantastic too, because we played well.

At the end of the game, when the girls found out they were division champs, they were flabbergasted. But they felt so good about being part of the team, I don't think the trophies could have made them feel any better. They won because they played well for the sake of the game, not for the trophies.

I heard a similar story from a soccer dad I know. His son's team didn't have a great season, but in the last game they were playing their hearts out, working really well together. During the entire game, parents on the other side were screaming at them, obviously hostile, while the parents on my friend's team were thinking, "It's just a game! Why are they getting so upset? What are they so intense about?"

My friend's team won the game 2–1. After the good game routine, when the boys came back to the sidelines and told their parents that the boys on the other team were crying, the parents looked at each other and said, "What's the big deal? It's just a game."

Then a woman from the other side came over with a box of trophies and said to the coach, "These are for you. You guys won the division." That's when they realized why the other team was so worked up. My friend said, "You know, I'm glad we didn't know. Even the coach had no idea we were in the running for division champs. If we had known, we probably would have been like those parents, and the kids would not have been able to play their best. This way they were just out there playing a great game, having fun— and they won."

Winning and losing with integrity
• *Losing with integrity*
There are only two ways a team can lose a game. The first is to play its absolute best and get beaten by a better team. The players are outplayed: they lose to a team that has more skill and is further developed. Can they applaud their opponent after that loss? That direction needs to come from their coach: "You were outstanding! You played really good soccer. I've never seen you play so well. You were fantastic— but they outplayed us. They were a great team." Can coaches

do that? Can coaches evaluate such a situation honestly? You can't just say something to a group of kids and hope they buy it. Is the assessment you give them honestly how you sized it up? It's important for players to receive this information from their coach.

☺   Did the team play really well and get defeated by a better team? If the kids played well, their coach needs to tell them so.

The second way a team can lose is by not playing well. If you lose to a team that you know you should have beaten—if you, as coach, can see all the holes in your team, and how the kids are not working together, not using what they've been taught in practices—then you know your team lost because the kids didn't play well. It's important to discuss this type of loss too. Just ask the players, "What did we do wrong?" They will know every time! They generally know better than the coach. I've asked that question and the hands go up everywhere. "We weren't as aggressive." "We didn't pass as well." "We weren't talking to each other on the field." "We weren't directing one another." They'll come up with every reason why they didn't play well. And they're always right, as far as I've observed.

☺   If you ask the players, they will know where they went wrong on the field—and they also know what they did right.

Imagine how team members feel when they know they've done everything right, they've played really hard and used everything they've been taught, but they lose anyway—and their coach puts them down for losing! The coach needs to forget about winning and losing long enough to evaluate the team's play and be able to discuss it honestly with the players—and not turn it into an ego bashing for the kids or the coach.

I once coached a brand-new basketball team. Only one of the eleven girls had ever played before. Skillwise, the players were terrible (and their coach wasn't a whole lot better). I'd played basketball as a kid and in high school, but it wasn't really my sport. This team went the whole season losing by huge margins. For the first three weeks we had zero on the scoreboard every game—against substantial scores for the opposing teams.

The first time we scored a basket, you would have thought we'd won the state championship! The kids jumped up in the air, screaming. Their coach screamed too and hugged them all! That excitement lasted the whole season. When the team finally won one—the last game, by two points—the girls were thrilled.

Every time these players went out for the next game, it was a new game. They never focused on their record—never wasted their energy thinking, "We've lost every game so far, so we have to win this one." The zero scores in the early games didn't matter.

Parents and coaches are the ones who attach meaning to winning and losing. The children begin to define themselves accordingly—they're good kids if they win and they're bad kids if they lose, *if that's what's important to the parents and the coach.* These same players can be proud of a good game whether they win or lose, if their parents and coaches give them positive support.

It's no fun getting beaten. It's not easy when you lose, but it's actually an important part of winning. Sometimes, the only way to become a winning player is to deal with a lot of losses. It's important to be able to say, "I lost. She was better than I, and it's fantastic she was that good."

As a child, when I would make excuses for losing a game, my father would always gently point out, "The fact is, you were outplayed, and there's nothing wrong with that. It's going to happen. You can't be the best all the time." If he hadn't made me face that, I might have just given up. If I'd had to be the winner all the time, I would have stopped competing.

☻ You experience a lot of losses before you get really good at a sport. You just have to humble yourself to take the beatings in order to become a winner.

• *Winning with integrity*

I had my back to the field at one game taking care of a player who was having a panic attack, so when I heard the cheering, I had no idea what was going on.

At halftime, I still didn't have a clue. I went through the normal spiel with the team about playing well, and then I focused on assigning positions for the second half. I never asked about the score.

After our team scored again, one of the fathers came over to me and said, "The score is 7–0, coach. It's time to pull your best players." That parent gave me a fantastic piece of advice!

A mother on one of our division's opposing teams told me their team had won its last game 7–0, although this team had not done that well before. During this winning game, one of the parents had suggested to the coach, "Maybe we should do something. The score's getting too high." The coach responded, "No, no, I want a shutout! Don't let them score! Don't let them score!" He was intense with the girls, pushing them not just to win but to keep the other team from scoring.

There is no justification in youth athletics for a team to run up a score. That parent was right to be concerned about the kind of coaching the children were receiving. It's a shame to put kids in this position, because they'll get enough of the play-to-win message later in life. We need to be more sensitive to the fact that the other team is made up of children no different from our own.

We don't have to give the opposing team a free goal, but we need to keep the game challenging for our own players. The strategy of putting players in unfamiliar positions is not intended to let the other team score; it is meant to even things out a bit. The girls still have to play their absolute best.

⊛   There are many ways of winning with integrity—that is, continuing to play a tough game without focusing on the score. Give the less experienced goalie some game time in the goal. Put special constraints on the players, such as requiring them to make five passes before they shoot or shoot with their off foot. Tell them they can't pass the ball until they have dribbled past a defender. The team members will continue to play their best, with the added challenge of concentrating on the weaker parts of their game.

"I want a shutout!" the coach had insisted. At that point, was it necessary to say anything at all? If he didn't want to put constraints on his players, why not just keep out of it and let them play! We are putting poison in the hearts of children in our charge by saying some of the things we say.

• *Coaching decisions*

I caught myself many times focusing on how to win the game. The score would be very close, possibly tied, and I'd think, "I should leave Michelle in because she can make the score" or "I should take Sandra out because I need someone else to go in who might have a better chance of making a goal." It's an unavoidable part of the coaching experience, and the challenge was to keep myself in check by being aware of it. It requires a conscious effort, in spite of the appeal of winning the game, to consistently make good coaching decisions for the kids—to be fair with playing time and to respond to each individual's need and desire to play, rather than focusing only on skill level.

It was tempting to leave in, or put in, the more skillful players if, for example, the score was tied with only five minutes left in the game or we were winning by one goal and I knew that by putting in a weaker defender we might lose the game. I struggled to stay conscious of the more important issue: I owed it to the team to be fair, and if that meant we took a loss, we took a loss. Before making a decision, I asked myself, "What is it going to say to the kids if I do this?" I found it was not worth it to give them a bad message.

⊛ As coach, I had to be consistent in trying to set a good example. Influencing the kids' moral values came first, not filling their trophy case.

The extreme of the winning/losing mentality—and the most damaging aspect—is when the coach excludes a kid from playing because she's not skillful enough. Fortunately, the rules of most recreational soccer leagues, up to a certain age of player, preclude this sort of treatment.

I have a friend whose daughter, Anita, is currently a junior in high school and plays on the varsity basketball team. Last year she was among the higher scoring players on the junior varsity team. This season, four games went by with Anita watching from the bench—she didn't play a single minute. After losing the first three games, her team finally won the fourth.

Immediately after that fourth game ended, in the midst of all the cheering and excitement, Anita's coach approached her to apologize for not having played her to that point in the season. Anita's mother had left the game in tears because she found it painful to watch her daughter go through another game sitting in uniform on the bench. When she asked her daughter later how she'd responded to the coach's apology, Anita said, "You know, I just didn't think it was the right time to bring it up, since the team was so excited about winning."

Indeed, it was not the right time to discuss something so important and so delicate. The coach's timing was very interesting. He may have felt genuine remorse about Anita's painful experience, but, no doubt, he was also extremely reluctant to discuss the situation with her for fear of confrontation. By offering an apology in the middle of the celebration, the coach avoided having an honest, open discussion about his decision.

As difficult as it is to justify the unfair treatment by Anita's coach, many coaches feel blameless in this sort of discrimination, especially those who focus exclusively on winning. In this case, an apology may have been more damaging to the player's confidence than saying nothing at all. The message in this apology is actually "I'm sorry about not playing you, but you're just not good enough to play on this team." That is very different from saying, "I'm sorry for not playing you, and I intend to change the situation because it's unfair to you."

⊛ When winning becomes all-important to a coach, the results can be tragic for a child. The damage that Anita's coach is causing to her spirit and self-confidence—and its effect on other areas of her life—is, in my opinion, an inexcusable coaching offense.

Sportsmanship

How do we teach our children to be good sportsmen and sportswomen? The coach's behavior goes a long way toward modeling good sportsmanship. It is also important how the coach handles instances of poor sportsmanship when they arise.

At the end of a game we lost, after the usual "good game" hand-slap routine and an exchange of "2–4–6–8" cheers, the other team lined up and did a cheer for our team that they had prepared. The girls' reactions were interesting: some were intrigued and thought it was kind of neat that they were doing a cheer for us and that they had worked on a routine; other girls felt they were "having their noses rubbed" in their loss.

The following week we enjoyed a 7–0 win. Toward the end of the game the girls on the sidelines came up with their own cheer. I was amazed at how fast they developed this routine (though it was annoying to some of their teammates, and they were told to "shut up"). Later, after the "good game" routine, our girls lined up and did the "Purple People Eater" cheer they'd made up—for the other team, they said.

I didn't want to squelch their enthusiasm, and I didn't want to attach meaning to it that wasn't there, so I decided just to observe it and let it go. I wondered, though, if we had lost, whether they would have done that cheer. Was it a cheer for the other team or was it a victory cheer for themselves? Both are fine. We need to cheer for ourselves, and we ought to cheer for our opponents. I didn't know which this had been, so I asked them about it at the next practice.

"I'm not saying this was a good thing or a bad thing," I began. "I'm simply going to raise the question: would you have cheered that cheer if we had lost?" They all said, "Maybe not." "I'm not going to tell you not to cheer. I just want to know, is it a cheer for the other team or a cheer for you?" "It's a cheer for us, because we were playing really well." "Okay," I said, "how do you think the other team feels if you do the cheer at them, if it's a cheer for you?" "Probably not very good." "Is there some way we can continue to cheer for ourselves, but keep it with ourselves?" They came up with a great solution: "After the high-fives, we can do '2–

4–6–8' for the other team, and then we can do our own cheer in a circle, for each other, and that way we're not rubbing it in their faces." They came up with a better solution than I could have given them—rejoicing in playing well rather than focusing on having beaten the other team. This is an excellent example of keeping competitiveness focused inward.

I witnessed an extreme example of outward-focused competition at an under-twelve boys' soccer tournament between two teams at very different skill levels. In the last ten minutes of the game, the coach of the winning team chose a strategy of "keep away" or possession soccer (keeping possession of the ball with no intention of shooting). When the losing team lost possession of the ball, one of the fathers in the stand called out, "Billy, next time just bruise him!" A father on the other team appropriately shot back, "That's some pretty poor sportsmanship, fella. I feel sorry for your kids." Apparently this had an effect. A minute later, when a player on the winning team received the ball, falling to the ground in the process, he managed to kick the ball to a teammate. While he was down, his opponent stood over him, raised a fist, and started to swing as if to strike. The player paused to look at his father, the man who had shouted "Bruise him." Luckily, there was no incitement from the stands this time.

I, too, feel sorry for those kids, being encouraged in a vengeful and hostile form of competition. Would this eleven-year-old boy have raised his fist at his opponent if his team had had a more civilized kind of coaching from the stands?

• *Opponents' mistakes*

At a tennis match you will never hear a crowd cheer for a mistake. They cheer for good points, and they're usually cheering for one player—but that does not mean they cheer for the opponent's mistakes. If a player hits the ball into the net, you will not hear them cheer. If she hits the ball out, you will never hear them cheer. They will be cheering when their player hits a great shot and the opponent cannot return it. Good plays, they cheer—but never a mistake.

I recall watching a friend's soccer game, when a girl on the opposing team inadvertently kicked the ball into her team's goal. Of course, all the kids on my friend's team cheered—they thought this was a great thing! It had been one up, and this poor kid kicks the ball into her own goal. The winners of the game are cheering because their opponents scored on themselves. I remember feeling very sad for the player who'd made the mistake.

My friend's coach would have been well advised to take the opportunity of bringing up the incident at the next practice and talking about a better way to handle it. Cheering for mistakes is something we, as coaches and parents, ought to discuss with the players to make clear to them it is unsportsmanlike behavior.

• *Opponents' injuries*

When I was holding tryouts for a competitive team, another coach in our recreational league paid me a very big compliment. One of his players was trying out for my new team. I recognized her as the goalie whose wrist had been fractured in a collision with one of my players. "I was really impressed when we played your team," the coach said. "When our player was injured, your team's response and your response were just fantastic. Your girls were really concerned about our player and you came out on the field to see about her. Some of your parents, too, came over to see if they could help. Your assistant coach offered us ice because we didn't have any. That told me something about you as a coach. You care about kids. You're a caring team."

The day before, he'd had a very different experience with his own daughter's first-grade team, when an opposing player deliberately threw his daughter to the ground. He said, "I told the coach, 'You've got to watch what your kids are doing.' The coach answered, 'You can settle up with me after the game if you want.' He challenged me to a fight! This was another parent, volunteering as a coach. The whole time they played he was yelling at these six-year-olds, getting angry at the kids when they didn't do something right." As he should have, this parent reported the incident to the soccer organization, and the coach was reprimanded.

Children naturally feel empathy toward one other. If they injure someone, they hurt inside. When a player has been injured, I first check on the person who's been hurt, and then I always go over to my players to see if they're okay, to let them know I know they're hurting too. I don't want to take away their concern, but I do want to help them understand when something is just an accident. When players can forgive themselves for causing accidental injury in a contact sport, it frees them to play a clean, competitive game.

• Teammates

In one game our goalie missed a ball that resulted in a goal and the defensive player closest to her turned and let her have it. From the sidelines we couldn't tell exactly what was going on. I could see words being exchanged, and it looked heated. Then, the goalie dissolved into tears. As she sat on the field crying, her teammate just kept going at her. I began to call from the sidelines, "Karen, quit talking. Get your head in the game!" but she kept at it. I found out later Karen had attacked the goalie with "Why did you let them score? You should have had that! You should have stopped that ball!"

We took care of soothing the goalie's bruised feelings, but there was no opportunity to discuss the incident. There were other teams coming onto the field, and parents rushing off for another game with their other children.

I brought it up, however, at the next team meeting. "I'm curious. When another team scores off us, where does the ball start? At kickoff, from what part of the field does that ball start?" "Fifty yard mark," they said.

"Okay, if we agree that it starts there, who does it have to go past to get to our defense?" "The offense."

"Okay, so now it's past the offense. I'm on the other team and I've passed all of the offensive players. Now, who do I have to get past?" "The stopper," they answered.

"Okay, now I've gone past the stopper and I'm flying! Who do I have to get past next?" "The defense."

"And how many defense are there?" "Two."

"Okay, now I'm past the defense. Who's left?" I asked. "The goalie."

"Who do I have to get past?" "The goalie."

"And if I do, I get the point, right?" "Yeah."

"So how many people did I get past? How many?" "Seven."

"So seven of you let me get past you. Seven. Is that the whole team?" "Yeah."

"Well then, ask yourselves how it would feel to be in the goalie box, standing there watching the ball go through your entire team and you're the last hope, and now it goes through you. And one of your teammates turns and starts yelling at you because you let it happen?" They all agreed, "That would be really terrible. It would feel awful." "What are some things we could say at that time?" "We could say, 'Good try. It's okay. It's not your fault.'" I said, "Well, can we start saying those things?" "Yeah." "Because if the ball gets to the goalie, who's responsible for it even getting there?" I looked around at all of them and I said, "Every single person on the team is responsible for the ball getting to the goalie box, not just the goalie."

After that meeting, the problem never recurred. In fact, from that point on, there was a lot of stroking and encouraging—a lot of positive reinforcement from team members to one another on the field. You could hear them saying,

"Good try," "Way to go," "Good shot!" It's amazing that such a simple question can so quickly raise the consciousness of the team.

• *Respect for all playing positions*
   One of the challenges in coaching young people is helping them develop respect for every position on the team. In recreational soccer, weaker players are usually put "on defense." These teams think of defense as a less important job. Offense is believed to be more important because offense scores. This attitude prevails on most youth soccer teams. The fact is, players in every position use both defensive and offensive skills. A defender is making an offensive play when she kicks it up the sideline to a wing, and a forward is playing defense when she pressures her opponent. Nevertheless, we categorize the various positions on the field as primarily offensive or defensive in their approach. At first, our girls didn't want to play defense, because they considered it an unimportant job. But the defensive positions became respected and in the middle of the season, a couple of players begged to be put on defense.

   It takes a certain personality to play defense and play it well. Our team had Mary, the smallest player on the team (and by appearance, the least powerful). But she was probably the most powerful kind of player for defense in a critical way: she was really, *really* stubborn. She would hammer away at the ball. It never mattered that the other player was a foot taller. When most players would shy away and give up, Mary kept pushing at the ball.

   A coach tries to find out in the practices what players have the type of personality suited to the job of defense. You put those players on defense, and then build up the position by letting the entire team know how important it is.

   The team doesn't do its best by having a great offense. The team does its best by having a working offense, a working defense, and a working goalie. Without good goalies and good defense, offense won't get anywhere. Our offense may score on every attempt, but then, with a weak defense, we get two goals scored against us. By showing each member of the team the importance of her particular position, you build up the entire team. If they all feel important and that they are doing the best job possible, winning and losing become less important.

• *Shaking things up*

I'd been concerned for quite a while that our players were getting a little too comfortable in their positions. I was having the kids play the same positions in every game. Offensive players played only offense and, with a couple of exceptions, they stayed with one position. The same was true of defense and goalies.

I also have strong feelings about running up a score. While I expected our girls to play their very best at all times, I never wanted to destroy an opposing team's morale by running up our score.

Finally, I had the perfect opportunity to shake things up—to keep the players challenged to do their best while keeping the score from getting too high. Within the first ten minutes of the game the score had reached 3-0, so I switched two offensive players with two defensive players. I did it right in the middle of the game, just as the referee was getting ready to blow the whistle for another kick-off. Neither the offense nor the defense was happy with me. Then I took out the sweeper—who is usually our strongest runner—and replaced her with one of the weaker runners.

At half time I had a team of very upset, if not downright furious, girls. "Kathy, what are you doing this for?" one demanded. "Why do I have to play defense?" another asked. After everyone had a chance to complain, I asked, "Does anyone have any idea why I'm mixing things up a bit?" "Well, since we're winning," said one girl, "you want us to play other positions so we can learn how to play them." Another added, "If we play other positions we won't be able to keep scoring, so the other team won't feel so bad." I explained that both statements were true, and that I wanted them to gain appreciation for what their teammates do every week, by playing each other's positions. One of the parents pointed out that the girls would also get a different perspective on their own position by playing the opposite position.

I then announced that Mary would play goalie. Although she'd never played that position in a game, she was good in practices. It quickly became apparent that I had neglected to remind her the goalie is allowed to pick the ball up! She proved equal to the double challenge, however, defending the goal using only her feet. I'll never forget the image of Mary blocking the ball with her foot, as an opponent kept hammering away at it. Finally, Mary, her foot firmly planted on the ball, put her hands on her hips, as if to say, "Enough!" Her opponent, confronted with this body language, stopped dead, while her coach screamed at her to kick the ball. I thought it was one of the funniest scenes I'd ever witnessed—probably because I'd been on the other side of that same body language so many times!

Heather, who had not played anything but defense, stuck it out on offense for a good ten to fifteen minutes, but dissolved into tears immediately upon being substituted. "I don't play offense! I'm DEFENSE!" she wailed. Christine, who had an extraordinary ability to dribble through an entire team of opposing offense and defense, was now facing her opponents as a defender—and was she angry with me! Lucia told her teammates, "Kathy doesn't know where to put me; I'm good everywhere." She hit the nail on the head. How nice, I thought, that she can know this about herself! There were even one or two who very happily went off to play positions they were not used to, and who honestly seemed to appreciate the opportunity to try something new, though I'm sure they would have chosen their usual positions if given the choice.

Most fascinating in this game was the way the parents and I, and the players in the sub box, responded to this change. It seemed that the parents cheered more for *all* the players, not just their own kids. I was able to be more positive and less judgmental. And for the girls in the sub box, it was a chance to see their teammates in a fresh light. We had few expectations of our players in the unfamiliar positions, so we were all able to appreciate their efforts regardless of the results. Len Oliver, a former U.S. Olympic soccer player and an A-licensed coach, has stated that an important element in building a healthy team is having each member play every position at least once.

As educational as this shakeup was, I knew it would require discussion at our next team meeting. As expected, there was much complaining and foot stamping, but I wondered whether the complaints might not be outweighed by a solid sense of accomplishment in playing their new positions, because we won that game 7–0.

• *Referees*

Kids are notorious for complaining about the calls referees make against them. They come off the field full of details about offenses committed by the other team, none of which were called by the ref. From the very first game, my approach was to respond, "I don't want to hear about it." "But they—" "I don't want to hear about it." "The ref didn't call—" "I don't want to hear about it." They were frustrated with me, but we (players or coaches) don't have the time or energy to spend talking about the ref. That's not getting our work done.

The first couple of games, any team goes through this— "That one hit me," "This one's picking on me." As soon as they start complaining, I tell them, "Too bad. That's life. This is a sport, you're going to get hit." "But—" "No. They're going after the ball, not you!" (There are players who will go after a person, but I have not seen a lot of it at this age.) After that, when the girls came off the field, they never said anything about the other team, or about the ref.

Dealing with opposing teams

A fourth component of team play deserves some discussion, namely, the opposing teams in the league. These other teams are, of course, made up of kids like those on your own team.

• *Cheering and heckling*

At one of our games, when the goalie of the opposing team stopped the ball, I heard one of our mothers remark, "Good save," and she clapped. Ellen asked her, "Why are you cheering for the other team?" The mother answered, "Because it was a good play. She had a good save there." Ellen turned around, clearly thinking about what she had heard. By displaying this kind of positive competitiveness, this parent was coaching me as well as the players in sportsmanship.

We don't encounter that kind of respect between opposing teams often enough. Much more common is the heckling of players and spectators by the opposing team. The coach's goal in this case must be to help the players disregard the heckling and remind them (as often as necessary) that they can't control the ref's decisions or the behavior of the other team—they can only control their own participation, and they need to stay with the game. Coaches remedy the feeling of victimization by empowering the individual player.

Just as complaints about the referee often become a chorus of griping, the feeling of victimization is also contagious. The coach has to interrupt that negative energy and stop it before it spreads through the team, by talking to the players at halftime.

In one game, when our players were taking a beating psychologically from the other team, they left the field at halftime focusing entirely on who did what to them. As they sat munching their oranges I gave them a pep talk: "You've got to stay with the game, not with a person. Keep your head in the game." "But they—" "I don't want to hear about it. I feel sorry for anyone who is so affected by another team they can't shake it off and keep their own standards and stay with the game." (These must have been my father's words, because a few weeks later I heard my sister, acting as substitute coach, give the identical speech to her daughter's team.)

Ideally, the coach will bring up the subject of heckling again after the game (especially if it was particularly abusive) and ask how the second half went. How did the individual players manage to stay with the game despite the verbal harassment (if they did)?

⊕ A debriefing allows the team to discuss the problem in a structured, supportive environment. Team members get to verbalize their feelings and hear each other's accounts.

I once sat in as assistant coach for a friend's recreational soccer team. That day, we were playing a very belligerent and hostile team and all the girls on our team became upset. One of them was reduced to tears by something her opponent said. Her teammates rallied around her in support, but they kept focusing on the negative experience itself.

It's not easy to turn negative energy around and make it useful, to turn it into productive energy. The coach insisted that the girls stop discussing the other team's behavior and focus on the game.

For Janis (the player most hurt by the experience), something more was required. She was sobbing and unable to go back into the game. I wasn't sure how we could take away that sense of victimization and empower her to deal with these verbal attacks. It seemed important to let her get through the experience, to stay with the feeling awhile, before she could get over it.

After a few minutes I went to talk to her. "You were hurt pretty badly out there. She really hurt your feelings." Janis nodded, still crying. "Is there anything you can do to empower yourself, to show her that you're not going to take it, that you're better than that, you're stronger than that? Show her that she can say whatever she wants to you, but you're going to stay in the game, you're going to take whatever energy is in you—and there's a lot of energy right now—and make it work in the game. Is there any way you can do that?" "I don't know," she said. "Okay," I said. "Go back in, and just concentrate on getting the ball out of the defense. Take everything you're feeling right now and just pound at that ball."

Janis went back in, and I was thrilled to see she was playing hard, being very aggressive with the ball. She played the rest of the game, and that team did not score against her. She was no longer a victim. She had turned that negative energy in a positive direction.

Coaches are also susceptible to heckling from the opposing team, especially from the other coach or the parents. I have to keep reminding myself that I cannot control what the other team does. I can't control the ref's decisions. I can't control the other coach's behavior. What I can do is keep my head in the game, try to maintain my own standard of behavior, and play with integrity and dignity. To do that, I need to keep myself constantly in check, change what I need to change to improve my game, and work to perfect the skills my team performs well.

• *Targeting a player*

There are times when a coach needs to take more direct action in dealing with heckling, especially when one of her players has been made a target by either the spectators or the players of the opposing team. A situation of this kind was described to me by the athletic director of a school in Connecticut.

The incident involved the middle school baseball team, which was made up of boys except for one twelve-year-old girl, generally considered one of the best players on the team. In an away game, against a much larger school, Shelley was pitching. As she began warming up on the mound, she was heckled by the spectators. The comments that most upset her were the requests for her phone number and the suggestions that she make herself available for a "date." The heckling continued throughout the game, but Shelley, though in tears, continued to play ball.

The question my friend had to address—and which we all need to address—is why the offensive behavior was allowed to continue, by Shelley's coach and the official, even though it was clearly causing distress.

The heckling went beyond the typical treatment of a pitcher, as it focused on the player's gender rather than playing ability and was completely unrelated to baseball—it was, in a word, sexism. This treatment is analogous to verbal abuse based on race. Can any of us doubt that sort of targeted heckling would have been promptly addressed, rather than permitted to continue?

The athletic director and one of the coaches met with Shelley to advise her on handling similar situations in the future. They explained that she had the power to call time, to stop the game and go over and talk to her coach. If there was no response from her coach, she should talk to the official. The official had the power to remove the spectators from the area, eject the offending players, or stop the game and award it to her team. She herself could end the game at any time (as the coach should) if any of the players are feeling uncomfortable or at risk. The point of the game, the director emphasized, was for them to have fun and be safe—not to be put in a compromising situation. Shelley responded that she would feel it was "her fault" if the game was ended.

When the director asked Shelley's coach, "Did you talk to the other coach or to the official? Why didn't you stop the game?" his response was honest and all too predictable: "Because we could have won."

Victims of abuse are often afraid to make trouble by demanding proper treatment. In sports, girls in particular are at risk. Most girls (and many parents, unfortunately) still see their playing on a team as a privilege, while boys regard playing as their right.

It's clear that game officials receive no effective training in handling heckling, nor are they prepared to stop a game for offensive conduct (even at the middle school level, where team standings don't count). There should be some channel through which coaches can complain about an official's inaction—and coaches *should* complain.

- **Spectators are witnesses**

A coach is simultaneously a teacher and a spectator. When the players are able to implement everything the coach has taught them, the coach can sit on the sidelines as a happy spectator. It is when players' skills fall short that the coach becomes a teaching spectator—and too often an angry one.

Obviously, young players' games will be fraught with errors: uncoordinated movements, forgetfulness, lapses in performance. Young athletes, after all, are developing athletes. In every game, they face opponents who challenge them at their current skill level. A winner in one game will be a loser in another. This is what sports are all about.

But, coaching *can* be frustrating! *Why can't they just do what I tell them?!!* It is the responsibility of parents to point out angry coaching. Address the issue as it arises. A private talk is best; you want to help the coach.

There are several effective and non-threatening ways of calling attention to a coach's missteps, of making the person more conscious of his or her actions:

- Ask the coach to repeat what she said: "What did you say just now to John?" Repeating the words should help the person recognize the emotion behind them.
- Point out the emotion you heard: "You know, you sounded angry when you said that to Alison." The instruction being offered by the coach may have been useful, but the emotion (anger, frustration, disappointment) is often what the player hears and responds to.
- Ask, "Do you think there may be a better way of saying that?" Even if the coach doesn't have a positive response, this may be enough to give her something to think about later.
- Ask directly, "Are you angry at Mary?" The anger the coach was expressing is that coach's emotion and she is responsible for it—not Mary.
- Get the coach to connect with the player's feelings. Try, "I wonder how it feels for Mary to be yelled at like that?" or "If you were Doug, how would you feel if . . ." or "I think you really scared [hurt, embarrassed, or humiliated] Vivian when you said—"

Spectators have a reponsibility to become active and supportive on behalf of the kids on the field or court. Parents have an obligation to help coaches become more supportive and encouraging mentors for their children. To witness the atrocious behavior of adults involved in youth sports and say nothing is an offense against the children.

CHAPTER SEVEN
Coaching Challenges

Issues of discipline

While managing movie theaters some years ago, I employed many high school students who worked to earn spending money. Some of them were fantastic employees who would do more than they were asked to do. One young man in particular stood out. Even the best team players will periodically act up, however, just to test the boundaries.

The theater had a clear dress code, which included an ironed white Oxford shirt. Anthony came in one day wearing an off-white shirt with very faint blue stripes. He went upstairs, put on his bow tie, and got ready to go to work as the concessions manager for the night. (That was a big job, as the person was responsible for $10,000 worth of business on a sellout night.) I asked him, "What are you wearing?" He started to give an excuse, but I cut him off. "No, uh-uh. Go. Good-bye."

I could hardly afford to lose an employee that night, but I said, "You're not in uniform. Go home." Anthony said he could go home, change, and come back, and I said, "If you can make it back, fine. But I don't care what you do right now. You know what the uniform is, and this is not how you come dressed to work."

Anthony ran home, changed into his uniform, and was back in time to work the show. I didn't say a word to him the whole night, giving him time to think about it.

When he approached me later in the evening, I said, "I appreciate your going home and getting into uniform. But don't ever do that to me again." He apologized and explained that things at home were a little tough. (I knew that he had some trouble at home, and I believe that's why he appreciated me. I paid attention to him.) I told him, "I understand that. If you need to take time off because you just can't deal with it on a particular day, all you have to do is tell me. But if you decide to come to work, you need to be 100 percent here. If you need a lighter job, if you want to be usher or doorman one night, just tell me. Whatever you need, I can do, but you have to tell me what you need. Don't force me into a situation where I have to do what I did today, because I will do it."

Anthony was a star player during his time at the theatre, but occasionally he'd have these check-ins with me. Today, he is a college graduate, serving as a volunteer in the Peace Corps. I am privileged to have remained an important person in his life over the past nine years.

Anthony and I did well together because I was consistent in setting boundaries and consistent with the consequences when he violated those boundaries. The same applies to coaches and players. I do not believe in taking power away from the players, but I am perfectly comfortable with discipline when it's necessary. I know that I have to do it, that I have to be consistent with rules as well as with consequences. I am very firm in the beginning. After that, the boundaries are clear. I am willing to spend fifteen minutes up front on basic discipline because I know that it can save me hours later on. Once the players get the message, we won't be going over the same point again.

• *Discipline: sraight talk*

For the most part, discipline on a youth sports team—like most discipline at home—is a matter of simply talking about issues of behavior and attitude. We do impose some consequences: wasting time in drills means losing time in scrimmage; straying out of the sub box means not going in when it's time to sub. But most issues are dealt with by firmly calling attention to the problem—not to humiliate anyone, but to make clear what is expected.

One occasion that comes to mind involved my first soccer team (assisting my brother-in-law). Our players won a game and, while doing the "good game" line-up afterward, the four girls at the end of the line spat on their hands before giving high-fives to the other team. I didn't see it, but I heard one of the mothers scream out, "Don't do that! That's disgusting!" Several other parents joined in, yelling at the girls, who were unfortunately out of earshot.

I asked one of the mothers, "What did they do?" When she told me, I headed right out onto the field. Up to that point I had let Mike handle most issues, because he was the primary coach. But he didn't know it had happened and I didn't stop to bring it to his attention. The girls were cheering for themselves and jumping up and down, yelling "YEA!" I stopped them and read them all the riot act. I said, "You don't ever, *ever* do that! What were you thinking? What kind of people are you?" I was very harsh, and that scared them. They had never heard me raise my voice or seen me get angry. They had only heard me cheer for them. Now I was letting them have it.

As I turned around to walk away I saw two mothers walking toward me, and I thought, "OH, NO!" You never know how parents are going to see things, and I'm always afraid they'll think I'm too hard on the kids. But one mother said, "It was a really good thing that you went out there, because somebody needed to do it and it couldn't be a parent. It had to come from a coach."

⊙ Often, players will put more stock in what the coach says, because they're somewhat desensitized to their parents and tune them out. As coaches, we have a responsibility to instruct the team in appropriate behavior.

A friend of mine, a former college basketball coach, discussed with me some of the difficulties male coaches have managing women players. What she observed is this: The coach sets limits, as all coaches do, and the players challenge them, as all players do—but instead of enforcing the rules, the coach gives in. Some coaches seem afraid that if they deal firmly with a female, she'll cry (and some do). Such coaches are ineffective because they don't know how to deal with the emotional aspects of coaching.

In one of our practices early in the season, we were doing a three-person drill called round-robin, in which the players had to keep running. If one person stopped running, the other two were unable to complete the drill. Dave told me he lectured one of the groups because they weren't running, pointing out one girl in particular. "And you know what she said to me? 'I don't feel like running today.' And she refused to run."

I immediately blew the whistle, calling everyone over, and had them sit in a semicircle in front of me. I was furious. I said, "Dave and I are doing our very best to give you the coaching we think you need to progress and be a contributing person on this team. When we tell you to do something, there are no ifs, ands, or buts about it—you do it. It is not up to you to tell us what you will and will not do.

"One of your team members just told the coach that she doesn't feel like running. He told her to run, and she didn't feel like running. You don't *feel* like running?" I scanned the group, making eye contact with each one of them. "I can't believe that any one of you has that kind of disrespect, not only for your coach, but for your team members. Because if you don't feel like running, you have just ruined the drill for two other members. You have made a decision to stop your teammates from progressing. If you don't feel like doing it, then at least have the respect for your teammates and the self-respect to sit out on the sideline.

"Don't come here and halfway do something. If you don't feel like doing what we have going on here, you need to quit this team. This is a major commitment, for Dave and for me and for you, and we have to stay committed. We said we would be here twice a week to coach you, and we will be here. There are days that it's not going to be easy for any of us, and hopefully there will be days that it will be fun for all of us. But we need to stay committed. I never again want to hear anyone refuse to perform a drill unless you are in physical pain." And I never did.

⊛   As coaches, women have an advantage: we are expected to show warmth and allowed to be firm.

• *Misguided discipline*

I observed a soccer practice of sixth-grade boys, in which one boy, Peter, kept interrupting the coach's instructions, unable to stay focused. The coach dealt with his interruptions every time by telling him to "Go run a lap."

The first time, Peter got up, groaning, "Oh, no!" and ran his lap. By the third time, the entire team was laughing. The other players continued practicing while this kid kept running laps. It turned into a big joke.

Peter got exactly the kind of negative reinforcement he was seeking. Unfortunately, he also ended up completely separated from the team, as he probably had been all season. He was obviously demonstrating an established pattern of behavior.

The coach could have handled the problem more effectively in a private conversation with Peter about the behavior he hoped to change. He could then put pressure on the other team members to help make the change happen, by creating incentives that focus on the coaching instructions.

Having the player run laps is nothing but a play of power—power*ful* versus power*less*. People have asked me,

"Why don't you make your players run laps when they get out of line?" I do make them run laps every day, but only for conditioning, as a team—never as punishment. In the case with the sixth-grade boys' team, the punishment became a kind of reward: Peter was being rewarded with special attention for disrupting the team. If a player is consistently apart from the team, he can never be a part of the team. I can't think of anything more disruptive than having somebody on your team that you feel is not really a part of it.

As forms of punishment, lap running and bench sitting only serve to exclude a player from the group. Twice in my coaching experience I've told a player, "I can't deal with this any longer. You go sit on the bench." Because I rarely used that approach, it was very obvious that the player was not, at that moment, part of the team.

The team needs to establish limits on its members' behavior, perhaps by making the whole team wait until their teammate is ready to participate. That is an old-fashioned approach, but often surprisingly effective.

• *Commitment*

One season, I was really challenged by one player in particular. Every time I called the team together she'd say, "I have to go talk to my mom," and she'd take off for the sidelines. Several times, even though I voiced objection, Mary ran off anyway. Finally I told her, "No, you will not go to your mother until six o'clock when our practice is over. Until then, your responsibility is to the team, not your mom." Mary was an extremely stubborn girl who would argue with just about everything I tried to do, and sometimes refuse to do it.

At the practice following this direction, her mother told me (in her daughter's presence), "Mary doesn't know if she wants to be on the team any more." "Is that right?" I asked Mary, who kept her head down. "Do you want to tell me what's going on?" Her mother explained that some of the girls were being mean to her, and "she's smaller than the rest of them, which is hard." "Well, I don't know about any of that, but I will tell you I came down on Mary pretty hard last week. Didn't I, Mary?" She still wouldn't look at me, but shrugged her shoulders. "Here's the deal," I said. "If you need to quit because I will not allow you to go to your mother during practice, that's fine. I'm not going to change my rules for you. I would like to see you stay, because I've got a position that only you can play—but only if you want to be a part of this team.

"You know, Mary, you're a really stubborn girl," (at this point she raised her head to glare at me) "and you're going to go through life with people telling you that's a bad thing. I happen to think it's a great thing, and it will serve you very well in life. But you have to learn how to use it. I don't want to change you, I want to figure out ways to really get that stubbornness working for us. I need a good defensive player, someone who will not let anyone get near our goal, someone who won't give up. That's you, my stubborn friend, and few of your teammates come close. I want you to stay only if you want to stay. You think about it, but you only have five minutes to decide, because practice begins in five minutes."

Within a few minutes Mary was on her way over to the other players to begin practice. Surprisingly, she never demonstrated an oppositional attitude with me after that—although that's not to say she wasn't a challenge in a dozen other ways!

What works with one person may not work with the next. With my headstrong Mary, I wouldn't think of trying to reach her with a lecture, because she'd never be able to endure the lecture long enough to get anything from it. She'd simply stamp her foot, cross her arms, and storm away. Being firm but calm, setting clear limits while using as few words as possible, is extremely effective with her. In fact, that is my preferred approach with all the kids, though there are certain ones who benefit from the hard, tough speech every now and then.

• *Tardiness*

One of my players told me that Sarah wanted only to play in the games and she wasn't coming to practice anymore. Indeed, Sarah was habitually late by half an hour. (I had to admire her consistency in that.) What made me furious was the fact that she would be accompanied—a half hour late—by her mother or father, and neither would offer any explanation. I struggled with whether I should address the problem with the parents, the child, or both together.

Finally I decided it was a problem for me as a coach, for her as a player, and for her teammates, who were mostly on time for practices. The next time Sarah showed up half an hour late, Jan happened to show up at the same time. Although Jan wasn't late quite as often, she too had a problem with time, so it gave me an opportunity to be tough without personalizing it. *You*, plural, is easier to hear than *you*, singular.

I explained that I recognized they had choices. Their choices were to be on the team or to quit. If they chose to be on the team they had no more choices, only responsibilities. They were responsible to themselves, to their teammates, and to me to show up to practices on time.

Then, in view of the fact that as recreational soccer team members, all girls got to play half of each game regardless of their participation in the practices, I decided to address the individual who was always late.

"Sarah, even if you continue to come late, I still have to give you equal playing time in the game, which means half the game. I've given this a lot of thought, and I've decided that I would have to put you where you would do the least amount of damage to the team. If you're not at practice, you don't know what your teammates are doing. You don't know the plays they've practiced, so you can't work with them in a game. Therefore, if you continue to miss important practice time, you'll play goalie for your half of the game. Goalie is a really important job, and I would hate to put you there, because you won't do as good a job as our regular goalies. But at least it's solo, so you won't be as harmful to the team as if I played you with defense or offense."

As that sank in, I changed gears. "But isn't it a shame," I asked, "that you and I are forced to think about where you'd do the least amount of damage to our team, when we should be thinking about how you'd help our team the most? You've got some good skills, especially footwork, that could really help us, but you need to be working with your team at practices to learn how to work together in the games."

Throughout this speech Sarah was staring straight ahead, her shoulders tense, poised as though she were about to cry. Part of me wanted to stop because her response was so painful to witness, yet I felt I had to forge ahead. Children give nonverbal cues to get what they want, but what they want is often not what they need. Sarah's nonverbal cues said, "You're victimizing me. This is too much for me. Be easier on me." I felt I had to show more faith in her than her own body language showed. I had to set boundaries that would maximize her potential to develop as a team player. Sarah had been focusing on herself, not on the value of the group experience. She hadn't understood that she needed the team and that the team needed her. This was a kid who thought she didn't matter.

While my lecture was obviously painful for Sarah to hear, and certainly not easy for me to give, she responded by coming on time the next few practices. More interesting, she began to speak more. She would ask other girls to pair up with her in drills, and she even started to tease me.

I sensed that Sarah's participation, and non-participation, was a sign that she believed she didn't count as a member of the team. (Not all cases of lateness have this underlying message. In some cases the individual feels she is exempt from the requirements of participation.) If we go through life thinking we don't matter, will we not encourage other people to disregard our thoughts, feelings, and desires?

The team experience can be a good way to improve a child's self image, but unfortunately it can also have an extremely powerful negative effect. Every coach needs to be on guard against the very damaging pattern of responding to potential victims by victimizing them. Perhaps Peter, who was given laps to run as punishment for his disruptive behavior, needed confirmation that he was fully a part of the team.

⊕   Coaches and parents must distinguish clearly between the kind of tough treatment that can build the child's self-regard, and the kind of tough treatment that merely vents the adult's frustration and damages the child.

• *Conflict among players*
Mary and Heather were on the same practice team, and the two kept fighting with each other. I repeatedly had to stop talking, while their teammates pressured them to quiet down. This had been a great attention-getting tactic for these two girls at the beginning of the year, but by midseason I had grown tired of the disruption. At one practice, halfway through the drills, Mary came up to me and said, "Can I please switch drill teams, because Heather and I don't get along?" "I really don't care," I responded. "No way." Since they were both defensive players, they would have to be able to work together in games, and practices offered them the opportunity to figure out a way to get along.

I told the practice captain to take her team aside and

142 Kathleen E. Donovan

find a way to resolve the situation. I was prepared, I said, to wait through the entire practice if necessary.

The drill team began by trying to come up with a lineup that would keep the two apart. After an argument about who would go ahead of whom, they finally decided that Heather would go first and Mary last—not realizing that after the first kick Heather would rotate to the back of the line right next to Mary! For a fleeting second I thought I should point that out, but I decided to let them handle the situation entirely on their own. Sure enough, someone noticed the problem and they went back to debating the lineup.

Ellen suggested several times, "Let's just call a truce." After a few more minutes of debate, Martina echoed Ellen. The idea caught on, the truce was issued, and the team returned to practice. I commended the practice captain for handling a very difficult job.

Individual challenges

A coach is not a psychologist. However, the individual personalities on the team can present interesting challenges that require tact and imagination. The coach needs to keep in perspective how his or her behavior has helped to create an existing team dynamic. By changing her own behavior, a coach can often dramatically change the behavior of her players.

In dealing with these challenges, the aim is not to "treat" the individual or sort out underlying psychological issues. The coach simply needs to come up with a way of getting past the difficulty, so the player can be fully a part of the team.

☺ When in doubt, keep in mind the first rule of coaching: "First, do no harm."

• *"This is coaching time"*
Elaine had a very defensive attitude, and it challenged

me to search long and hard to discover a way to coach her. The first couple of times I tried to correct her moves during a drill, I was shocked to hear her explode at me, "I KNOW! I was doing that!!"—so shocked that I simply couldn't respond.

The next couple of times Elaine screamed at me, I seriously questioned myself and my tone of voice, my attitude. Was I angry at her for not doing the drill right? Was my tone harsh or accusing? What else might be going on in her life to cause her to react in this way? I reached a point that, before I said anything to Elaine, I would rehearse it. I'd find the gentlest, most supportive way to approach her. I'd start my comments by pointing out what she was doing well, and then show her how to improve. Even so, as soon as I got to my suggestion for improving—BOOM!—another explosion.

After a few practices, with several of these outbursts each time, I became angry and struck back. "God, Elaine," I snapped, "what is the problem here? I'm just trying to show you how to do a turn with the ball!" This exchange began to resemble a shouting match, and I felt I was being sucked into a battle of wills. I went home after practice that evening ready to explode. I prayed hard that night to find a way to deal with Elaine that would allow her to develop her game and be proud of it instead of feeling attacked when criticized.

I decided to talk with Elaine privately before the next practice. I began by asking, "When I correct you or try to show you something, why do you think I do it?" Looking me steadily in the eye, she said, "I'm doing something wrong." "Try again," I said. "You're trying to make me do it the right way," she shrugged, still keeping intense eye contact. "Okay, keep going. Anything else?" "You want me to do it better," she said with a little grin.

"Elaine, you're getting closer. May I tell you what I'm trying to do?" I asked, deliberately giving her the opportunity to say "No, don't!" "Okay," she shrugged again.

"You know, Elaine, I look at you and I see all this potential, and I know you can do more than you're doing. I know we can improve the skill you're working on, so I think, 'Well, I'll just show Elaine this next piece.' It's not because I think you're doing something wrong, but that you're doing something so well, I feel we can perfect it.

"Everyone has a time when they're maxed out on a skill and have reached their full potential, and I would never want to push them beyond that point. If I'm trying to teach you more, it's because you're showing me that you can do more. I'll stop when I see that you're maxed out on that skill."

Remarkably, Elaine never broke eye contact through this entire speech. We were clearly connecting, for the first time in the two weeks we'd been working together.

"So," I continued, "from now on, if you start to get defensive—which seems to be your immediate reaction—I'll just say these words: 'This is coaching time.' That will be your cue to let me show you something to improve your game. That's all I'll say: 'This is coaching time'—and then you can let me help you. Is that an okay way to work together, Elaine?" She gave a big smile, and another shrug of her shoulders. "Okay," she said.

At the next few practices, when Elaine got defensive and I said, "This is coaching time," her response was to tighten her jaw, grit her teeth, and endure. Then, after two weeks of my consistently responding to her defensiveness with, "This is coaching time," she would grin and nod for me to continue. By the end of the season, Elaine would actually ask me to watch her practice a skill I had corrected: "Wait, is this right?" I was glad to finally have her permission to coach her!

• *"Take care of me"*

For some players, the gentle, caring approach is not the best way to go. I'm afraid I have rewarded some players' weaknesses with tremendous empathy. I have allowed these players to create—or rather, I have created with them—a pattern of behavior that can easily pervade other areas of their lives.

With one player in particular, this pattern was especially difficult to break—remarkably, for the same reasons that made her a great athlete. As an athlete, Theresa tended to practice a skill until she got it right. She always looked for new and more skillful ways of playing the game. She was tenacious and didn't give up easily. Moreover, she had an unbelievable ability to focus—a particularly helpful trait when she played goalie. Ironically, these strengths also helped to keep Theresa locked into the cycle I call, "I'm weak. Take care of me."

It was exasperating to observe these impressive strengths and feel forced to spend so much time and energy dealing with Theresa's focus on her weaknesses. I realized that Theresa and I had created this problem together.

I had several players who arrived at every practice with some ailment that precluded their doing the mandatory lap running. The aches and pains vanished, I noted, during the scrimmage. With Theresa, however, the inevitable sore throats, stomach aches, and breathing problems were not a way of getting out of running laps but gave her an excuse to stay close to me. All kids love to hang out with their coaches, but rarely to the point that they prefer standing on the sidelines with the coach to practicing with their teammates.

Theresa and I were locked in a dynamic that reinforced her perception of weakness and my sense of importance. Just as a perception of one's weakness creates fear, a perception of one's strength creates confidence. If we were so successful at bringing out the weakness-reward cycle, we could surely be successful at bringing out Theresa's strengths.

In order to break this cycle, I knew I would have to be-

gin ignoring Theresa's pleas for attention. I consulted
Theresa's mother, who shared my belief that the problem was
one of perceived rather than actual ailments. (A physician
had performed a stress test to rule out exercise-induced
asthma.) I shared with Theresa's mother my intention to take
a firm approach in correcting the problem, which she supported.

✪   In any situation dealing with a child's perceived injury
    or incapacity, it is essential to determine whether there
    might be an underlying physical condition or a compli-
    cating emotional problem. The child's parents should
    be consulted and their cooperation obtained before at-
    tempting to correct the behavior pattern.

The next time Theresa complained of "runner's stitch"
or some other pain, I told her to keep running. When the
complaints escalated to whining, my voice showed my impatience: "I said, keep going!" When she collapsed in a ball
on the field, I simply said, "Theresa, get up and get moving!
I don't want to hear any more about it!"

Theresa's mother was present on the sidelines, and
Theresa would then go sobbing to her. Her mom would simply say, "Go tell your coach." It was fortunate for both
Theresa and me that her mother trusted my judgment that
we were doing the right thing.

I knew that success depended on consistency. Dave
handled the situation the way I was handling it: "Get moving." I don't know whether to laugh or cry as I picture Dave
facing this little girl, not yet ten years old, who was sobbing
that she couldn't breathe. It went completely against Dave's
gentle nature to look straight at this hysterical child and say,
"Theresa, keep going." As I watched from the sidelines, my
heart went out to both of them.

Their laps completed, the players crowded in to grab

their water bottles, and almost every one of the fourteen girls ran to take water to Theresa before they had a drink themselves. *God love them all!* Dave said to me later, "Did you see how the whole team went to help her?" The team evidently felt compelled to provide her the caretaking that we, the coaches, were withholding. At that point, he agreed with me that we had to stick it out and break this "Take care of me" pattern.

I had spoken privately with Theresa earlier that day so that she would know what to expect. A short time later, however, she announced that she couldn't do a drill because her leg hurt. I got the drill started and then took her aside. Using the caring voice Theresa had grown to appreciate so, I said, "You know, I'm trying really hard to bring out Theresa, the strong, powerful athlete. And you're trying hard to show me how weak and fragile you are. We all have weaknesses, but we have many more strengths. The weaknesses are there for us to try to overcome, to show us ways to get stronger and more powerful.

"It's frustrating for me to deal more with your weaknesses than your strengths. You're fast, you learn quickly, you're strong, you're incredibly skillful—which makes you a great athlete. Do you get what I'm saying?" Theresa nodded. "I'm going to continue to do what I'm doing, so that you and the whole team get to know the powerful person you are. I will not stop, so you need to decide whether you want to work with me. Okay?" Theresa nodded, and we went back to work. She fell in with the drill and, for the first time in several weeks, when I praised her skill she actually heard me. She turned around and gave me a gorgeous smile. God love you and keep you joyful, Theresa!

About half an hour after our talk it was time to scrimmage. As this is my favorite part of practice too, I never miss my chance to play. During the scrimmage, Theresa and I collided heavily and she went flying. I kept going, and she immediately jumped up and yelled, "Hey!" and came flying at me to steal the ball. Two days before, she would have collapsed in tears after a hit like that.

From that day on, we made steady progress in phasing out the damaging behavior and bringing to the surface her strengths. I saw once again the value of consistency and commitment. Of course, these things are useless without an honest concern for the players themselves. Coaches must remain aware that relationships with the players contribute to our lives too and give us the opportunity to grow and develop along with the kids.

• **Competition between teammates**

Grace had tremendous speed, real agility, and beautiful skills, but she held herself back. She'd work really hard to win the ball, only to move out of pressure with a half run, instead of taking it away at top speed. It was as if she was offering the opponent another chance at the ball.

Whenever I put Grace and Elaine on opposing scrimmage teams, Elaine would say, "Oh, no, please, *please* don't make me play against Grace!" When the two were together for drills, Elaine would say, "Oh, good, I get Grace on my drill team!" But if they were going one-on-one, it was "Oh, no, not Grace!"

Finally I asked Elaine, "Why do you complain when I put you opposite Grace?" (The answer might have been obvious, but I made a point of asking the players that sort of question as a way of making them more conscious of what they were thinking, saying, and doing.) Elaine said quietly, "She's so good," and she walked away.

I decided to give them a few weeks of practicing apart. Playing together, neither Elaine nor Grace was free to shine— Elaine because of her conviction that she would never be as good as her friend, and Grace because of her belief that it was not okay to be better than her friend. Dave remembered hearing Elaine say to Grace, "Grace, before you came I was the best player on the team."

During those few weeks Grace became more aggressive and seemed to enjoy competition. When she won the ball, she worked hard to keep it.

Elaine was obviously competitive too, or she would not have fixated on Grace's ability. Her competitiveness had become so outwardly focused she no longer valued her unique skills. She was a fantastic goalie and had a natural aggressiveness on the field, gifts that Grace lacked. With the separation, Elaine was able to focus her attention on developing her own game.

CHAPTER EIGHT
"Nothing Gold Can Stay"

Recreational soccer remains a social activity until fifth or sixth grade. At that point, the more competitive or athletic players will generally move on to higher level teams.

Coaches need to understand that these changes can be heartwrenching for young people, who are at the same time facing the challenges of middle school and early adolescence. Part of the coach's responsibility—just as important as forming the team in the first place—is managing this transition and providing a sense of closure. For most players, there will be some unhappiness at making the change, but they will be better prepared to deal with the situation if their participation in their old team is properly acknowledged.

Divisions emerging within the team
• *The team talks it over*

At a team meeting, Lynn said she was getting "a little mad at some people" because they were not coming to practices on time. (Sarah had just shown up fifteen minutes late again.) "And when they're here," she told the group, "they're not really paying attention and participating. When we're doing the drills, they're sitting on their ball, or talking." This opened up a can of worms. Right away, everyone's hand shot up. Lynn added that the non-participating kids were being "kind of bratty."

I stopped her to sum up the first points she had made about people talking and not paying attention. But when I got to the "bratty" part, I had difficulty interpreting what she meant, so I asked, "How are you defining 'bratty?'"

Lynn explained, "While the rest of us are practicing really hard, they just don't want to do anything." Susan added, "I think that *bratty* is not being willing to participate. When the rest of us are practicing, they're not even trying. It's not really fair to the rest of the team because when they're goofing around it holds up all of us."

Christine jumped in. "When they're part of a drill team and it comes time to do the drill, they don't know what to do because they haven't been paying attention, and so they can't do the drill. All of us look bad because they don't know what to do."

Liz said, "Sometimes we get out there, and a couple of us have been paying attention and know what to do, but the others haven't been, or they don't care. So they go out and goof around or do the drill sloppy. So all of us look bad. And then you think none of us know what to do, and so you stop everything and end up repeating everything when really we know what to do. It's just a certain few who are goofing around. So really it's just wasting everybody's time."

Lisa had an interesting perspective: "I play piano, and I get these magazines. I was looking at the back of one the other day and it said how it's not fun to practice, but you need to practice in order to keep playing better. And that's sort of related to soccer. We need to keep practicing in order to play better. The drills may not be all that fun, but we're playing better because of them."

Finally Mary spoke up in defense of those who goof around. "I was reading a magazine, and it said that kids do sports because they want to play and have fun. That's the most important thing, to have fun. Kids don't really want to do the exercises, but they want to have fun."

"That's a good point," I said. "Having fun is what this is mostly about. But let me ask you something. When you guys were doing single-digit math problems in school, and you figured out how to do them, they became kind of fun, right?" They hesitantly nodded. "Now, suppose your whole class went on to do double-digit adding and subtracting, and you stayed on the single digits. They would be working hard at it, and it's not so much fun but they finally get it. You're still having fun playing around with your single digits. Then the rest of the class goes on to multiplication. You're still doing your single digits. Is it still fun?" They all laughed and said, "No way! No!" I said, "Do you see my point? We can continue to do the same stuff, and not move up to these harder drills—but while everybody around us is improving, we will stay at the same level. Will that still be fun for you?" They chorused, "No."

"So what you're all saying is that there are a couple of our teammates who are hurting us in two big ways. The first way is that we're not able to practice as much, so we're not learning as much as we could. The second way is they are robbing us of our scrimmage time. That gives us all something to think about."

⚽   The players themselves asked to talk about the issue, without my bringing it up or even suggesting it was a problem.

It's important that the players were able to say what they felt and discuss their grievances without pointing fingers or humiliating other players. That is something they seem to do of their own accord, always referring to "some people" instead of naming specific individuals. I commend them on their diplomacy.

• *Zen and the art of team maintenance*
When I told a friend about this extraordinary meeting, she asked, "Now that you know all this, what are you going to do about it?" "Nothing," I replied. Not every problem that comes up needs fixing. The players would do the work just by saying to the group, "This is what I notice. This

is how I feel." Keeping things out in the open is a solution.

How divided are we?

Our recreational team had been dividing since the beginning of the season. There seemed to be two distinct groups. Perhaps the players were divided according to the schools they attended—or because some had played together longer. Maybe they were divided because of friendships they'd formed before coming into the game. Or was the division because of skill level? One group appeared to include players who were not particularly athletic, while the other group developed soccer skills quickly and performed better every day.

Perhaps the two groups reflected a difference in interest level rather than skill level. Body language spoke volumes. Heather planted her feet, put her hands on her head and waited for the ball to come all the way to her feet. Ellen spent practices sitting on her ball, breaking twigs into small pieces. Sarah was consistently late to practice.

There were a couple of higher-skill players who shared some of the characteristics of the I-don't-really-want-to-play group. They were disruptive in practices and chose not to run in the drills because they "didn't feel like it." During scrimmages and games, however, these girls would play hard and would gladly have played entire games without a break had I allowed it. On the sidelines they followed me, begging to go in (the inspiration for the sub box, discussed in chapter five). In their cases, the problem was one of attitude rather than lack of interest or skill.

• *Athletic skill and athletic interest*

As the season progressed, the difference in skill level among players became remarkably clear. I wondered if some players' lack of improvement reflected a lack of athletic ability. This was a major concern for me. I tried hard to concentrate on positive reinforcement for skills gained and avoid correcting mistakes or overdoing the instructions.

Toward the end of the season we stopped giving instructions altogether. We were not teaching new skills, and further direction in the old ones seemed punitive for the girls who couldn't master them.

• *Serious or social?*

It seemed likely that the less motivated players were affected by a combination of factors: lower skill level, frustration, and less athletic interest.

I heard one mother say, "I'm athletically able, but I just don't know why anyone would get excited about running after a ball!" I remember saying the same thing for years about golf. It's slow, and who would want to walk around for hours hitting that tiny ball? Now I'm addicted to this maddening game, even though I'm lousy at it. For me, golf is a social activity. I get silly and laugh at my errors in the company of a friend or two, preferably without any serious golfers around. Yet, put me on a tennis court with someone who clowns around the way I do on a golf course and I'd want to wring her neck!

This was a good frame of reference for me to use in gauging our soccer team. I think most of the players in the less motivated group were having a blast out on the field. They laughed at themselves and each other, enjoying the game and being with their friends. Practice, however, was a drag for them with a coach who was becoming more serious about skills and drills.

I began playing tennis when I was about five years old. My father, a serious tennis player, would not let me play on the court at that age because it would be disruptive to others. He taught me how to play by hitting the ball against the school wall. He patiently readjusted my grip, standing behind me and guiding my arm, helping me swing the big wooden racket at the tennis ball as he dropped it. We did this over and over, day after day and week after week, until I was about seven, when we began to play fairly regularly on the tennis court.

By about fourth grade I started to get the hang of the game and I wanted to play all the time. I wanted to learn everything there was to learn, using my Dad's helpful tips to improve my game. I was perfectly content to practice my backhand, my net game, overheads and serves, because I was beginning to recognize the feel of a good shot. I would watch tennis matches on television and want to play immediately afterward, rushing out to mimic the pros' shots as best I could. It was exciting to realize that the subtle readjustments to my grip and swing could make such a remarkable difference in my game. As a fourth-grader I was playing tennis seriously because I had the bug, not because this was what my family did. None of my friends, however, played tennis seriously, and after a few attempts to play with them, I confined myself to playing with my Dad and my brothers and sisters, or simply practicing on my own at the old school wall.

My golf game helped me understand the group of girls who play soccer for fun. My tennis experience helped me empathize with the more serious soccer players. The serious players wanted the drills. They delighted in improving their ball skills. In practice they went over a drill repeatedly, asking me to check whether it was right and then improving upon it. They introduced new skills they'd picked up from parents or friends or from watching higher-level games, eager to share with their teammates. They wanted to move onto more serious play, with teammates who were equally passionate about the game.

- *Torn in two*
     Once again I found myself faced with a semicircle of

mirrors, each reflecting a piece of me. Our two groups of players sat side by side, as one team: twelve girls who had worked together for about eight seasons—twelve soccer players who mirrored, individually, the varied approaches I myself take to different sports. They represented the serious tennis player I once was and the silly social golfer I am today.

As I looked around at that circle of beautiful young women, I could see all the most personal pieces of myself, the strong parts and the fragile, the large disappointments and the even larger hopes.

Just as the team itself was dividing, becoming increasingly frustrated on both sides, I was feeling torn as well. It was difficult to organize productive practices—go too slowly and one group was bored, step it up and the other group would put on the brakes. At one practice, a girl from each of the groups had taken hold of one of my arms and they literally pulled me in opposite directions at once—a nice metaphor for my feeling of being torn in two.

It had become clear to me that my greater frustration was with the less serious group. I began to be angry with their failure to participate, their habitually disruptive behavior, and their unwillingness to try new skills. I'd gone over and over it in my mind: if I could happily clown around through nine or eighteen holes of golf, why was I taking the soccer practice so seriously? Why not take coaching more lightly, as simply a healthy social activity? Why was I approaching it as a challenge, the way I took on tennis at the age of ten?

The decision to divide

Throughout my life I have developed a passion for many different sports, and soccer is one of them. I'm athletically inclined, and my passion easily develops into serious competition. But that's me. For others, sports are simply fun.

Those individuals just enjoy the social interaction. They enjoy attending practice and playing around with the ball. They enjoy running around on the field and playing with their teammates. And they enjoy the positive reinforcement, because it is perhaps the only place they get unconditional support from their peers. If the coach consistently works at teambuilding, the players' interaction is positive, supportive, and encouraging.

During my last season as recreational soccer coach, there was talk of some players trying out for competitive teams. One of the parents approached me about taking the whole team "up" to the competitive league. I dislike the use of the word "up" in this situation. It suggests that recreational soccer is inferior. The choice of switching levels of play should be presented as a set of alternatives, not as a kind of graduation. It's the choice between right and left, not up and down; green and blue, not first and second.

I'd been struggling for a while with the issue of whether to form a competitive team. On the one hand, I felt I needed more of a competitive challenge. I like to see athletic progress; I like to see the players developing their skills, developing their understanding of how to work as a team. I felt that I needed to have players who wanted to do more, players who really wanted to improve.

Although I hated to say goodbye to any of the girls, I knew there were those who couldn't take the discipline of a competitive team. But I knew that I couldn't just pick half of the group to start a new team. I was also worried that I might not be interested enough in competitive play to commit to the hard work.

There's a lot of pressure in a competitive league. The quality of play increases, attention to the game by parents is greater, and competition between teams is more intense. And unlike recreational soccer, in the competitive league there is more incentive to win. If a team finishes among the last few teams in the division, they are dropped to the lower division, or back to recreational if they're already in the lowest division. The play is very competitive and coaches push harder.

I finally realized that for myself and my own growth and development, I had to continue coaching with the committed soccer players, the ones with a passion to improve in the game. I wanted to push my limits as a coach. To continue coaching a divided team, facing constant resistance and dissension, was draining for me and unfair to both groups of players.

• *When to break the news?*

I first informed the parents of my decision to start a competitive team. Some of them asked that I hold off telling the players until after our last game. But the reason the parents wanted me to wait to break the news is the very reason I needed to tell them sooner rather than later. The girls and I were a team. I knew they were attached to me, as I was to them. Hiding the news and springing it on them at the very end of the season was an idea I found deeply distressing. I knew it wouldn't be fair to any of us not to have enough time to prepare emotionally for the last game we would play as a team.

The parents' concern was that the girls would be further divided if Dave and I talked about our plans. I felt they were underestimating our team and its potential to resolve uncomfortable issues.

I ran the question past Denise, a friend's fifth-grade daughter, who is also a soccer player. She was emphatic in her response: "Oh my god, that would be terrible! If you waited until the last game, at the party, it would be awful because it's like you're just dumping them." "Wait a minute," I defended myself. "I'm not dumping them, I'm just moving on to something different." "Yeah, but if you tell them on the last day, it's like saying, 'Well, thanks you guys, it's

been a great year, but I won't be coaching you next year, so
see ya!' They thought you were a great coach all year, but if
you do that to them on the last day they're going to say, 'Oh
great, then the whole year was a waste.'" "Wow! Why would
the whole year be a waste?" I asked, thinking this was a little
over-dramatic. "Well, because they really liked you and
trusted you, and they thought you liked them too. But then
you just tell them this, so they think, 'She was really a fake
the whole time.'" "So I definitely have to tell them soon."
"Yeah, I mean right away, like at your next practice. Then
they have time to think about it, they can talk to you about
it, they can call you if they want. And they'll know this is
the last time they'll play with you, so they can really do their
best."

All this from a girl only a year older than the players
on my own team! I was struck by the idea that the whole
year would be a "waste" if I didn't play it straight with
them—as if a bad curtain call would cancel out the whole
show.

• *Closure*

Taking Denise's advice, I prepared to tell the team at the
next practice.

As always, I began with a team meeting, everyone sitting in a semicircle. Since this meeting was so important to
me, I set up cones, evenly spaced, and had each player sit in
front of a cone, so that I could see and hear each of the girls.

Broaching the subject immediately, I told them I was not
going to be coaching them in the fall, as I had decided to
coach a competitive team. The players quickly changed from
laughing, giggling girls, full of energy, to a group of blank
faces. I asked, "Any thoughts, feelings?" Susan spoke first:
"I feel like someone just dropped a big rock on my head."
Liz added, "It feels like lightening, like being struck by lightening." Ellen followed with "Gosh, I feel like I was just hit

by not one ball but two." Shari pulled one knee up to her chest and kept her face partly hidden the whole time, never saying a word. Heather's eyes welled up.

None of them took their eyes off of me. As adults, when we're presented with information that is sad or painful, we generally do whatever we can to focus our eyes on something other than the speaker. We glance at the clock, play with our pens, rock back in our chairs, look out the window, or straighten the papers in front of us—and then we change the subject. The kids had not mastered these defense mechanisms, which left me completely vulnerable to their emotions, unable to use my adult avoidance tactics. If I tried to look away, there were twelve pairs of eyes keeping me in the moment. I told them it had been a very difficult year for me and that coaching had been a huge challenge. "You have no idea how much you helped me by letting me coach you," I said, my voice cracking. A roomful of adults might have shifted uneasily in their seats, scanned the room, picked imaginary lint off of their sleeves, or exchanged anxious glances until someone managed to change the subject. But those twenty-four eyes remained on me. No one said a word, allowing me to recover so I could continue.

I explained how torn I had been about whether to tell them now or wait until the last game. Susan said, "That would have been terrible. This is sad, but at least this way we know, and we can—" "In a way it's bad because we wanted you to stay as our coach," Christine said, "but in a way it's good because we know we only have two more games together. So now we can play our best so we can show you how good we are." Liz said, "Some people can't play well when they're sad and depressed. It's like when your parents go away on a business trip, you really miss them and it's hard to do anything."

"That brings up a good point," I agreed, "because I'm one of those people who doesn't perform well when I'm upset about something. I think some of you picked up on that last week." "Yeah, you were kind of depressed last week," someone said. "You're right, it was difficult for me to practice then, so I really know what Liz is talking about. It might be a little rocky for us during the next two weeks, so let's just try to be gentle with one another. If you're not performing well, and I get on your case, just say these three words: 'Kathy, let up,' and I'll let up." Susan said, "You'll *try* to let up!" "No, I'll let up, I promise," I reassured her.

Heather, who had been driving me crazy with baby talk for the past month, finally spoke—still tearful—in the voice of a mature young woman, "You know, I've just found out my music teacher is leaving, and now this, and I've had a lot of losses this year. My best friend is leaving, and we had to put my cat to sleep, and now this." Liz joined in, "This feels like when my cat died. It feels just the same. It's really sad." Others brought up losses they had experienced.

Lynn, with a tear on her cheek, summed up: "It's like nothing gold can stay. I mean, really good people come into our lives, and they're like gold, but then they have to leave. My best friend moved away and I was really sad when she left, but now we write letters to each other so she's not completely gone. We have to make the best out of the good things while they're here." Christine said, "Maybe you could give us your address, so we can write to you and send you postcards." "Of course," I agreed, "I'd love to get letters from you." Liz said, "This is really hard because you've taught us everything about soccer and now you're not going to be teaching us." "We did learn a lot together, didn't we?" I said. "And next year, you'll be using those skills on the field, and hopefully for as long as you play soccer." The girls nodded. "So you'll be taking a part of me with you. Every time you play soccer you'll be using some of what I taught you." I also told them I would like to be invited to their games, and asked if they would come and cheer for me in my games the next year.

Susan, with astonishing maturity, pointed out, "I think we should be happy for Kathy, because she said this was a really tough year in her life and now she's doing better so she can coach a competitive team. And that's really good."

After our talk a few of the girls asked me to attend their end-of-year concerts and recitals. And one asked if I would still come to the summer soccer group that Dave was setting up. "If Dave calls me, I'd love to come and play," I answered, making clear that I would not be the one in charge—since I would no longer be the coach.

Poor Dave sat there during the entire meeting and didn't say a word. I wondered how he felt. Afterwards he looked at me and said simply, "Whew!" "I'm glad I told them," I said. "You're right, it's a good thing," he agreed. "Cats dying, teachers leaving, friends moving. Whew!" We both laughed. It must have been hard for him, as the only male in the midst of so much raw emotion.

I had the girls do their running after the meeting. I hoped that running would give them time to process their feelings and get centered again. Surprisingly, Sarah asked to be the pace setter. Running is not one of her strengths, and I admired her courage.

Following that practice, Liz told me about a dream she'd had a few weeks before. In her dream she played soccer in high school and then in college, and I was her coach. I was "always there." Then she went on to play professional soccer, and suddenly I wasn't there. "I kept looking for you but I couldn't find you anywhere. You left me and I didn't know why."

Ten-year old kids are very intuitive. As we get older, we tend to dismiss our intuitive knowledge, to rely on more objective sorts of information. We learn to judge people by their words rather than by the indefinable sense we have of them. I believe the most reliable sort of knowledge is gained by intuition. Rather than pushing that sort of information aside, we need to learn how to evaluate it and put it to use.

In the two weeks leading up to that practice, there must have been plenty in my behavior for a sensitive participant to notice and respond to, as Liz clearly had. I had tried to honor the wishes of the parents who wanted me to wait to tell the team about my decision, but at great personal cost. I was avoiding eye contact and personal encounters. I didn't start practices with a team meeting, because I found it too difficult to face the girls.

I had begun to wear sunglasses to practice (as a protective shield I suppose). Christine must have understood this. At the beginning of one practice she took the sunglasses from me and, quite uncharacteristically, simply refused to give them back! I was annoyed and uncomfortable, but nevertheless interested to observe just how exposed and vulnerable I felt without my sunglasses. Christine kept them for the entire practice and happily returned them at the end.

In retrospect, I realize that I purchased my first pair of sunglasses about two months after the assault. I had never worn them previously, and I recognized that I was using them as a screen, as protection against anyone seeing my insecurities and emotional turmoil. By taking them away, Christine was in effect forcing me to trust the team with my feelings.

I had been prepared for the question "Can we try out for your competitive team?" But I didn't want the girls to focus just yet on the new team. I wanted them to make their decisions carefully regarding what would be best for their own level of interest in soccer, without being drawn along by the group's reaction to losing their coach. In answer to the question of having tryouts, I simply said, "Yes, but I really don't want to get into that right now. For now I want to focus on the fact that our team is playing its last two games together."

Tryouts

Holding tryouts for a new competitive team presented a major challenge. Every aspect of the decision to form the team was loaded with potential conflict and emotional fall-out.

Dissolving a team is painful enough for a coach—having to divide a group that has cheered, supported, and encouraged one another—without adding to it the agonizing task of choosing players for the new team. For me, this is without a doubt the most distressing aspect of coaching children. How do you choose one ten-year-old but not her best friend? How do you tell a child with whom you have worked so intensely side by side for two or three seasons, or more, that she's just not good enough for your new team? How much more painful it is when you know this child has poured her heart and soul into practicing, so she can join a more competitive team!

Once I had decided to form a competitive team, my first instinct was to allow any of our girls to join the new team, provided they were willing to make the commitment to longer and more intense practices. I quickly discovered that some of the parents found this approach unacceptable, and I was pressured to choose players more selectively and objectively by holding a judged tryout.

I yielded to pressure, and with my co-coach, Dave, I held structured tryouts, with three experienced coaches judging skill level. Entrants were given numbers, which they wore, and they performed different skills at each of three judging stations. At the end, the judges tallied up the scores and chose the fourteen highest scores for the new team.

• *How objective are tryouts?*

Choosing team members strictly according to tryout skills seems objective, but it does not take into account the variable of tryout anxiety, which was severe for two of my better players. Nor does it take into account the variable of coachability, for which these same players certainly deserved to be rewarded. Conversely, two players rose to the occasion and performed better than I had seen them play all year.

This created a real dilemma for Dave and me. We were very tempted to override the judges' selections in favor of the two coachable players. Nevertheless, we felt we had to be honest with the families who had brought their kids to try out for what they understood to be a new team, selected in fair tryouts.

I was physically sick over one of our players. Lucia's disciplined, she's supportive of her teammates, and she has a real passion for the game. She has all the attributes of a great team player, yet she was not among the fourteen selected for the team. I was sure that her heightened anxiety at the tryouts had interfered with her performance—but there was no objective way to factor that into the scoring.

The tryouts were fair, honest, and objective, but only as far as soccer skills were concerned. The subjective criteria, such as desire, discipline, enthusiasm, commitment, determination, supportive attitude, and ability to accept correction—in sum, what I call coachability—were not part of the judging equation. These character traits are more important than skill level could ever be, because I am coaching children, not a college or an Olympic team—although, even at advanced levels of the sport, coachability can be an important factor in a team's success.

It is clear to me in retrospect that holding tryouts was a mistake. I never again want to injure the spirit of a great young athlete, as I fear I did this time, by disregarding the greatest component of the game—coachability—in favor of skill.

⊛ Instead of having tryouts, a better approach might be to simply invite interested players to practice with the team, so that the coaches can see and evaluate the whole player—the social, psychological, and athletic dimensions.

• *Taking it in stride*

I wish I had paid more attention to the considerable pressure these ten-year olds feel as they try out for different teams and have to decide between them. The kids have big decisions to make, and deciding is made all the more difficult when parents have their own agendas.

One mother told me that her daughter was really excited about the idea of joining my competitive team, but that it was a big decision and she wanted her daughter to take some time to think it over before committing herself. That was a very sensible approach. Kids can get so caught up in the business of tryouts and the excitement of being accepted they sometimes forget the responsibility they would be accepting. Having them sleep on the decision is generally good advice.

Another mother called me, after her daughter had accepted a spot on our team, to say that they had discovered a new team starting up close to home. She was concerned that Sonia had too little contact with the children in her own neighborhood and, at the mother's request, her daughter agreed to try out for the new team.

The mother went on to say that friends had advised her not to tell me about the other tryout until she knew her daughter had made that team. I asked, "Why would anyone tell you to do that?" She explained that they feared my response might be, "If Sonia doesn't want us, we don't want her either." I assured this mother that I had encouraged the players on my team to look at other teams and try out for other coaches. I also expressed my complete agreement with her about the importance of Sonia's making friends in her neighborhood. I told her that if she could give me an answer in the next two days I would hold a place for her daughter.

The intensity the parents brought to this process was a big surprise to me—and a little scary. I can't imagine being a ten-year old having to make decisions at that level. A kid's soccer team is an avenue to help young people develop, so the process shouldn't become a problem.

Who are the kids becoming in the process of playing on their teams? What life skills are they gaining? Who are they becoming in their community? These are more important questions than will she make the team!

EPILOGUE

At the heart of my coaching endeavor, always, are the memories of my dad. By becoming a coach I was able to bring my father's voice back into my life when I needed it most. Of the dozens of coaches I've had in various sports throughout my life—many of whom were wonderful, others not so great—my tennis coach has always stood out. I'll forever be grateful that this exceptional coach was my dad, and that I had the benefit of his patient, good-humored coaching almost every day of my life, from childhood to early adulthood. His love for me and for the sport shone through in his coaching.

With the patience of a saint, Dad would call me over to the net. "Let me see how you're holding the racket, sweetie." He'd readjust my grip and have me practice a swing or two before we'd return to play. On days when I consistently hit the wood rather than the strings, sending the ball everywhere but within the white lines, he'd ask, "What are you thinking about?"—in a tone of voice that was merely curious. "I don't know." "Well, it's not the ball, because if you were watching the ball hit your strings, you would be hitting it in. So let's forget about everything else for now and just watch the ball hit your strings." After a few rallies, I'd hear, "Beautiful! Now you've got it." His persistent, respectful coaching had brought me back to a very quiet, mindful game of tennis.

There were times when I'd slack off out of frustration. I wasn't playing well, and the problem would snowball because I'd get so upset with myself. Dad would try to bring me back to the game by saying, "Remember, the battle's never over until the last shot is fired. Try not to get discouraged, honey." Sometimes those words were enough to nudge me back to mindfulness—at other times, they'd throw me into an internal fury that felt beyond my control. I knew, however, that I had a choice, and I was responsible for the choice I made: mindfulness or fury.

When I was in my twenties, my dad lost his battle with ALS (amyotrophic lateral sclerosis), also known as Lou Gehrig's Disease. I remember a colleague of my dad's telling me at that time, "Do you know how much your father loved you, Kathy? We used to love to hear him talk about your tennis. He'd say 'God, you should see the way she hits that ball!' He really loved you."

I have no doubt that the daily experience of being coached by my dad, with so much thoughtfulness and love, allowed me to become a coachable person in other areas of my life.

The decision to coach a girls' soccer team was an important choice I made along the road to recovery from the assault. The challenges were formidable, both physically and emotionally, but together the team and I made enormous progress. And I knew that I was never alone in my endeavor. I consciously strived to stay in line with God's will, knowing that I would do the greatest good for the children and for myself with His guidance.

This is a book not about what I have accomplished as a coach, but about what my Coach has guided me to create. In working with these young girls, I consistently prayed for solutions, guidance, and direction, but above all I prayed, "God, help me love them." Now, finally, my prayers are what my dear mentor, Sister Kathleen, once told me are the most beautiful of all prayers: prayers of thanksgiving.

Biographical Note

Kathleen E. Donovan served in the Peace Corps as a primary health care worker in the Philippines (1984–86). She served as International Program Director for the YMCA in Japan (1987–89), supervising as well as teaching in their English-language program. She had several years of management experience in the movie theater industry before obtaining her master's degree in social work at Catholic University (1994). She currently works as a social-skills and communication-skills coach in the Washington, D.C., area, to assist children with various learning and behavioral challenges.

In the course of recovering from a near fatal assault she suffered in 1993, Kathy drew on her life-long love of sports, as well as her extensive experience in teaching and counseling, to become a coach of girls' soccer and basketball teams. *Conscious Coaching* presents a communications approach to some of the problems that arise in youth sports, offering a variety of innovative coaching and team-building techniques, as well as insights into the psychology of both coaching and learning a sport. The author also offers a candidly critical assessment of some prevailing approaches to youth coaching.

Written originally as a personal coaching journal, *Conscious Coaching* is presented in a direct and readable style, focusing on specific incidents and personalities encountered in the course of coaching. Kathy vividly records her own observations, reactions, and difficulties in dealing with each situation. The result is a fascinating and sometimes moving personal account that will become a valued resource for anyone involved in youth sports.